Getting Started Riding a Motorcycle

Walter F. Kern

Getting Started Riding a Motorcycle

By Walter F. Kern

This book is dedicated to my children:
David, Steven, and Susan

Contents

Preface

This book was written to provide motorcycling information for new riders to make them safer riders. It's also intended for returning riders who have been away from motorcycling for many years. It's based on articles I published while I was the Motorcycles Guide on About.com and also during my current assignment as Editor of Motorcycle Views, which I founded.

I am astounded to see so many motorcycle riders dying in traffic accidents, some close friends of mine. Some were seasoned riders with complete knowledge of how to ride safe on the road, yet they still died in motorcycle accidents. Others variously had little or no motorcycle safety training, suffered a lack of knowledge about motorcycle operation, wore inadequate riding apparel including helmets, or misused drugs and alcohol. It's hoped that this small book will help to save a few lives, unnecessarily wasted on the highway.

As you read this book, realize that I am intentionally repeating and stressing certain points that I feel need to be understood and remembered by my readers. Motorcycle safety is very important. Without proper training, you'll have an increased chance of serious injury. Therefore, you're going to read a lot about how to be safe in this book.

The appendices contain a glossary of motorcycle terms, a set of motorcycle How-Tos, and a packing list for those long trips.

Chapter 1

Getting Started Riding a Motorcycle - My Story

It was August of 1993 -- the year of the great Midwest Mississippi floods. I was stopped behind a car towing a trailer. A Wyoming state road employee was holding a stop sign up ahead. I was on my 1990 Honda PC-800 motorcycle. My wife, Jane, was immediately behind me on her twin PC-800. We had ridden up from Cody after an overnight rain had stopped. We were on our way to Bear Tooth Pass. After waiting for five minutes, I could see cars moving ahead. I pulled in the clutch, jammed my left foot down to engage first gear, let out the clutch, gently rolled on the throttle, and began following the trailer ahead of me. That was to be a mistake.

Almost immediately I knew something was wrong. The road surface was becoming soft. Now it was mud. Then I realized that the drivers ahead of me had misinterpreted the signal of the person holding the sign and had taken the side of the road that was under construction. This mistake was no big deal for the cars but it was a giant problem for anyone riding a motorcycle. My bike was now swerving. Then I thought of Jane behind me. I looked in my rear view mirror just as she fell...

It was only an instant in time before I reacted but before that, my mind raced recalling the events that got us here.

It started in 1989 when we traveled back to our hometown in Illinois. We always stayed with Jane's sister, Carol. Carol's husband, Jack, was a Renaissance man. He had no college degrees but was a self-made man who undertook everything with a passion for excellence. He loved motorcycles. He had a complete machine shop in his garage to maintain his own bikes. At that time he had two BMW motorcycles. He and Carol had traveled everywhere on those machines, even to the top of Pike's Peak. I had always harbored a secret desire to ride but had never acted on it. On our last day there we were standing in the garage seeing off Jack and Carol's son who was packing up his motorcycle to return to Chicago. I stood there looking at the bike for a long time. Suddenly, I knew that I had to learn how to ride before it was too late.

On the way back to New Jersey I brought up the subject and to my surprise, Jane was enthusiastic and said she had always wanted to ride but thought I would never go for it. When we got back, we acted quickly. Jane immediately found someone at work who had a used 400cc Honda for sale. We bought the bike, got our permits and scheduled our road tests. We still didn't know how to ride. I had heard about the Motorcycle Safety Foundation (MSF) classes that were taught at a local college. We enrolled in the 3-day course and passed. Now we needed a second bike and it just had to be a new one.

By nature, I'm a pretty easy going guy and very conservative. I'm not into intimidation. So, the first time I screwed up enough courage to walk into my local motorcycle dealer looking to buy a new bike for Jane, I could just feel the intimidation as I stood there among those sparkling chrome machines. I could hear the subdued tones of the salesmen and customers talking about motorcycles using language I could not comprehend. There were rows and rows of machines all lined up like silent soldiers. I was afraid someone would come up to me and ask me to leave for being so much out of place. Oh yeah, I was intimidated by it all, but I was not going to leave.

We had decided that Jane would get the first new bike. She got a 1989 Honda Shadow VLX. We found that the people at the dealership were really nice people. In fact, we began to see that almost everyone we met was nice. The media image of motorcyclists did not seem to be true. Shortly thereafter I traded in our first bike on a new 1991 Honda Nighthawk 750.

We started going to rallies but had not joined any clubs. Jane needed to find other women riders who could act as a support group. We quickly found the Spokes-Women Motorcycle Club. Jane joined and I became an associate member. Shortly thereafter, I heard about a group called the Polar Bear Grand Tour. This group had 400 members that rode throughout the winter to points within NJ, NY, PA, and DE. I figured there was no way Jane would want to do this. However, when I brought it up, she was all for it -- so long as we could figure out a way for her to stay warm in the 20 degree New Jersey winters.

On Halloween in 1992, we sat around a table in Lewes, DE at a Polar Bear gathering when one of the women said, "How would you and Jane like to join us on a trip out to Cody, Wyoming next year for the Rider Rally?" Well, that was something to think about. We knew that we would never know whether we had the ability to go on a long trip unless we tried one. And the fact that we would be going with experienced motorcyclists made the decision easier. However, we needed different bikes to do this 6000 mile trek. We ended up with twin 1990 Honda PC-800 bikes. We did a lot of planning into 1993 and ended up with four bikes and five people going.

We had a lot of fun on this trip and learned a lot. We found that we could ride 500 miles in one day if we had to. We met many colorful riders and swapped hundreds of stories -- I'll save those for another time. We rode through the desolate Sand Hills of Nebraska where you can ride 50 miles without seeing another vehicle. We rode into Sturgis, SD where the giant Sturgis Rally was being held. (The picture shows me waving from the rows of motorcycles parked on Main Street.) We headed to Cody, Wyoming for the Rider Rally. Cody is the next town out of Yellowstone Park. We toured Yellowstone on two occasions and almost froze to death. Our Polar Bear electric clothing saved us.

While at the Rider Rally we missed the guided tour of Bear Tooth Pass. Jane said she just couldn't ride 6000 miles and not see Bear Tooth Pass since we were only a few miles away. So we started out on our own. The roads were good for a while but then I saw traffic stopped ahead and I started slowing down...

Suddenly, my revere was ended as I leaned forward to look in my mirror to see what happened to Jane. She was sprawled in the mud about 50 yards behind me. She and the bike had parted company. I then became aware of my own situation. I was still moving but I needed to stop. Hopefully, I wanted to stop upright. All I could think of was the training I had received in my courses and the tips I had received from other riders. I gradually began applying the brakes gently so as not to lock up any wheel. I had to steer so as not to allow the bike to fishtail. Somehow, I got the bike stopped and my feet down in the mud, upright. I slowly turned the bike to the left and across the gravel median to the other, paved, side of the road and headed back up the hill toward Jane. My tires were coated with mud and they were slipping. I didn't know if I would make it back without falling down myself but, somehow, I did. I parked on the side of the road and moved Jane's bike across the median to my side. Jane was OK but covered with mud. We always wear leather jackets and gloves, and wear helmets so Jane had no perceptible injury except bruising. We just had to get all the mud off her and the two bikes. We decided not to continue to Bear Tooth Pass and headed back to Cody where we spent the rest of the day washing down everything and relaxing.

We were able to ride down to see the Grand Tetons before we had to head back East. Somewhere along the way, our party of five had split up. We were going to have to ride the 2500 miles back to New Jersey on our own. When we got back and related our stories, our kids couldn't believe our adventures. Our daughter, Sue, said,

"Most parents worry about what their kids are doing. In this family, the kids worry about what the parents are doing."

After six more years of riding on two wheels, we each switched to 3-wheels - trikes. She rode a white Honda Gold Wing and I rode a red Honda Gold Wing.

We took a few more long rides after 1993. We continued to attend the Americade Motorcycle Rally in Lake George, NY every year in June. It's the biggest touring rally in America. We didn't have any motorcycle accidents in the 19 years we rode together. Maybe it's the training we received or the fact that we picked the times we rode to be safe. I don't know. I do know that the thousands of good times we had in motorcycling would not have been possible without taking that first step into the unknown and deciding to learn to ride.

Note: In August 2008, I lost Jane in an automobile accident while she was on vacation with her friends. She was greatly loved by her family and friends. She was a unique individual, always ready to test her boundaries and have fun. We had 47 years of great memories together, especially 19 years of riding motorcycles. Now, I'm moving on in the wake of her legacy, trying to continue to live my life as I know she would want me to. Of course, that will continue to involve motorcycles.

Chapter 2

How You Can Learn to Ride a Motorcycle

I receive a lot of questions from people who want to learn how to ride a motorcycle but don't know where to start or what steps they should follow. There is no magic process to learn how to ride. Every rider follows a different plan of learning. The following is my plan to learn how to ride a motorcycle should you choose to follow it.

Motorcycles

Motorcycles are 2-wheel vehicles patterned after bicycles but with much heavier frames.

Early motorcycles were actually bicycles fitted with small internal combustion engines. There was a gradual evolution as numerous motorcycle manufacturers entered the market and competed against each other.

A motorcycle works using a complex interrelated set of parts controlled by both hands and feet and requires coordination and skill not required to drive an automobile. In fact, people starting to learn to ride a motorcycle without ever having ridden a bicycle or driven a stick-shift car, may be at a disadvantage when trying to learn to ride.

Motorcycles have been a part of transportation for a very long time. They were once much more prevalent than automobiles until such pioneers as Henry Ford found out how to mass produce cars at a price below that of motorcycles. Over the years, motorcycles have come to fit a variety of needs beyond basic transportation. Today's rider may use a motorcycle for commuting or everyday use. Some riders use their motorcycles for basic transportation and don't own a car. Some ride a motorcycle as part of their lifestyle. Some ride motorcycles only on weekends. Some ride on lengthy cross-country tours. Some even travel around the world on adventures.

Motorcycles have evolved to include 3-wheel vehicles called trikes. Motorcycles are sometimes fitted with a sidecar to allow whole families to enjoy motorcycling.

In the United States, only one company, Harley-Davidson, has been able to survive over 100 years, producing models every year since its first model in 1903. In fact, to most non-motorcyclists, the words "motorcycle" and "Harley-Davidson" are used interchangeably.

Although many motorcycle brands exist, the most prominent besides Harley-Davidson are Honda, Yamaha, Kawasaki, Suzuki, BMW, and American made Victory.

Although Indian began producing motorcycles in 1901, two years before Harley-Davidson, they have had a history of closings and re-openings. In 2003, Indian closed its factory in Gilroy, CA. The 380 Indian employees at the plant were told that a deal with a new investor had fallen through. In 2006, there were again rumblings that Indian might be coming back. Shortly thereafter, a new Indian company was formed to continue the Indian name. They have hopes of producing a new Indian motorcycle too. On April 19, 2011, Polaris announced that it had acquired Indian.

Who rides motorcycles?

A motorcyclist can be created at any time. It's often a matter of timing. Some learn when they're young and grow up with it. Others get the urge later in life. The bug bites them and they can't get rid of it. They're hooked. Some want to learn but are constrained by family members who declare:

> "Motorcycles are dangerous. I know somebody who almost got killed on one."

Maybe it's your wife or husband who doesn't want to see you get hurt. More likely, it might be that you now have kids to care for and your spouse announces:

> "Motorcycles will just have to wait."

Everyone has a story why they can't ride but wish they could. The truth is that if you have the bug within you to ride a motorcycle, you will find the right time to take up motorcycling. No amount of pressure from friends, family, or society will deter you from participating in motorcycling. Look for the right time and "Go for it!"

If you are stumped by any motorcycle terms you've heard trying to learn about motorcycles, be sure to check out the Motorcycles Glossary in Appendix 1.

How to get started riding a motorcycle

Making the decision

You'll know when decision time is near. I don't have to tell you here. One day, you see motorcycles only in the background. You view some riders as irresponsible, riding noisy machines that only serve to awaken you from a sound sleep. Darn those bikers! Then suddenly on the next day, it's as if a new window has opened and all you can see through it is the motorcycle of your dreams and all you want to do is get on that machine and ride off over the next hill and never return. What a transformation!

Sportbikes as a first motorcycle

In my motorcycle forum, we get many people seeking help in learning to ride a motorcycle. Usually they come into the forum having been "bitten by the bug" and want advice on buying a sportbike as their first bike.

We try to set them straight and turn their thinking around. They need to first take a training class offered by the Motorcycle Safety Foundation (MSF). Then they need to get a cheap bike to learn on for six months to a year. Then they can think about getting that sportbike or other model.

Getting trained to ride a motorcycle

I once took a completely unscientific poll that indicated that 79% of motorcycle riders were self-trained or learned to ride a motorcycle from a friend or family member. In the old days -- 20 years ago -- that's the only way you learned. There were no widespread courses available. Such is not the case today.

I cannot emphasize this enough: You must take a formal course given by the Motorcycle Safety Foundation (MSF) or by a school that uses the MSF's methods and whose instructors have been trained by the MSF. These courses are usually given over two and one half days with both classroom instruction and field exercises. Motorcycles are provided as part of the class. You just show up with long sleeves, jeans, gloves, and heavy boots. You don't even need a permit.

They supply the rest including the helmets. The beginner motorcycles used for MSF training are small - 250cc usually. During the field training, they take you step-by-step, introducing you to the motorcycle and teaching you how to ride it.

Some states even provide a motorcycle endorsement on your license after you successfully complete the course. However, my personal opinion on this practice is that you don't know enough to ride safely after completing this short class. The class exercises are conducted in parking lots and the bike rarely gets out of second gear. You need to get lots more practice with an experienced motorcyclist before you venture out solo into high-speed traffic.

The classes teach you how to ride a motorcycle, but more importantly, they teach you street survival skills. You need to know the proper way to ride a motorcycle in traffic and avoid situations where you are most vulnerable. People laugh at me when I say it took me a solid year of riding under all kinds of conditions before I felt comfortable riding a motorcycle. Your time will be different but it will take time. And of course, you never want to feel so comfortable that you let down your guard and expose yourself to undue risk. You do need to always remain alert.

Even if you are already an experienced rider, I guarantee that you will learn to be a better, safer rider if you take one of these classes. There are experienced classes for those who have already completed the first course and/or have some riding experience behind them. Some states even have intermediate classes. These additional courses are conducted with you riding your own motorcycle.

What motorcycle should I get and what should I wear?

Getting that first motorcycle

You want to start off with a simple, cheap, beginner motorcycle and be prepared to see it fall over a few times while you get used to riding it.

If you're not familiar with all the types of motorcycles, check out Chapter 4, Motorcycle Types, that describes and shows 10 motorcycle types, one of which may fit your riding style best.

Just be sure that the bike runs well, has good tires and brakes, and is insured. After you've taken the MSF course, you'll need to get lots of practice riding. Find an experienced motorcyclist to go out with you and act as your mentor for a couple of months. Ride around in your local area first avoiding busy roads and heavy traffic.

Gradually ride on the country roads, the highways, and then the high-speed roads as you gain experience. Try to be aware of all you learned in your MSF training and put it into practice. You may have a few spills as you ride your motorcycle. Most of these should be at low speeds or parking lot situations and will not injure you. Your motorcycle may suffer some cosmetic damage but that's why you bought an inexpensive bike to learn on.

At some point in this training, if you haven't already done so, you'll have to take a motorcycle road test offered by your local Dept. of Motor Vehicles. After passing this test, your driver's license will be endorsed. You are now motorcycle-legal.

If you're lucky, you'll get through your practice sessions successfully without damage of any kind. You may suddenly feel that the bike you bought and thought was so huge at the time, now appears tiny and you want something bigger. It happens to everyone. Probably you will be able to sell your starter motorcycle for what you paid for it. I did.

Clothing needs

You will see a variety of attire for people who ride motorcycles. Some non-riders object to the black leather image as being too outlaw. They've seen too many bad biker movies. Whether you want to believe it or not, there are certain predominant styles of attire depending on the brand of motorcycle. I'll let you observe these for yourself.

Clothing is for comfort, protection, and safety. Every rider wears either a T-shirt or turtleneck sweatshirt. These are usually emblazoned with pictures, sayings, or other motorcycle-related text.

The first thing you have to protect is your head. Now I know this is a controversial subject and that many groups have expended great effort to lobby states and other governmental agencies for the right to choose whether they want to wear a helmet. I choose to wear a helmet and I recommend that you wear a helmet at least for the first year while you are learning to ride.

You should wear gloves specially made for riding. If you fall and hit the road, most likely, your hands will hit first. Let the road rash be on your gloves, not your hands.

You should wear hard full-length motorcycle boots. Sneakers are not a good thing. Boots limit foot and leg injuries should you fall.

I prefer a leather or fabric jacket with vents. I started out with a leather jacket but now prefer a fabric jacket. Currently, I'm wearing a FirstGear Kilimanjaro jacket. During the summer, I open the vents to allow air circulation. During the winter, I put in a liner to retain body heat. Riding down the road in the summer in the 90 degree heat will dry your skin quickly. A jacket will retain skin moisture and cool you. If you wear leather and you go down, you will thank the day you decided to wear leather and save your skin.

Leather pants or chaps are great if you want further protection. I prefer chaps when it starts to get cold. Many riders like full riding suits either of leather or synthetic material.

If you like winter riding, I recommend heated vests, heated gloves, and possibly heated socks if it really gets cold. Also, a full bib-style suit such as you might use for skiing is desirable. There are also complete heated apparel that includes vests, pants, gloves and boot liners that are interconnected together and controlled by temperature controllers. I also own one of these by Gerbing.

The reality is that riders will ride with almost anything on, sometimes offering practically no protection at all. It's your call but I hope you'll think about what I've recommended here and make an informed decision.

Into the world of motorcycling

Clubs and support groups

Many motorcycle riders are solitary and shun groups. Other riders like to be around people who ride the same brand of motorcycle. Still others choose groups that welcome all brands of motorcycles. There are many groups, associations, and clubs to choose from.

There are also many women's groups. Most of the women's clubs welcome male riders as well but emphasize support to new women riders.

I wholeheartedly recommend that you join the American Motorcyclist Association (AMA). This group has over 260,000 members and monitors the rights of motorcyclists. There are also many ABATE groups (American Bikers Aimed Toward Education) that offer training, fellowship, and support motorcyclists' rights.

Rallies

After you have some experience riding, you will begin to hear about the various motorcycle rallies. You should get a buddy and go to one that's not too far away. Most new riders will start out by taking a day-trip to a rally. Then maybe, they'll try one with an overnight stay. Riders may then want to spend several days at a large rally and opt to reserve a motel room or a campsite for the duration.

You may find one that you want to visit every year. The Americade rally in Lake George, NY is an example. The Sturgis Motorcycle Rally held in early August each year in Sturgis, SD, is a mecca for motorcyclists. The attendance at Sturgis has exceeded 400,000 in some years. Other large rallies are Daytona Bike Week in Daytona Beach, FL and Laconia Motorcycle Week in Laconia,

NH. Many riders prefer the smaller rallies where anywhere from 200 to 1000 show up. There is a rally for you.

The second bike

You'll get the urge for a second bike very soon after you've been riding. You will find that you see motorcycles everywhere. You'll begin to recognize them. Your friends will ride in with new bikes and you'll long to have something new yourself. The bug is biting even stronger now. As I mentioned before, you will probably be able to sell your first bike for what you paid for it.

At any rate, you will be buying a second bike and you'll probably start to assess how you ride before you buy it. If you like the more aggressive riding style, you may want a sportbike. You may want something to commute on and choose a standard bike. You may like to just be seen around town and go for a cruiser. Others may have been out on some long rides to rallies and want a sport-tourer or a touring motorcycle. You have more decisions to make.

Venturing out into the world

After you've had a year or two of riding, you may start to venture out more into the world. You may plan to take a cross-country tour or ride to a far-off place like Alaska. You may become a member of the touring community. Some can't get enough of riding and think nothing of riding from New York to Chicago for a good cup of coffee at a favorite café. Some have ridden around the world. Others participate in individual tests of personal endurance such as the Iron Butt Rally or the Four-Corners run. There is no limit to the distance you may be compelled to go.

Also, riding long distances does not mean you have to be on a Honda Gold Wing, a Harley-Davidson dresser, a BMW touring bike, or other heavyweight tourer. Anyone can tour on any size bike and it's done all the time. Again, you have to make the decision what you want to do and what kind of a rider you want to be.

I hope I've been able to give you a flavor for what you are in for once you make that decision to ride a motorcycle. You may never be the same again. Hopefully, you will grow with the new experiences you gain and be safe while you're riding. Whatever you do, continue to learn how to be a better rider and enjoy yourself. You CAN ride a motorcycle. More importantly, you WILL become a motorcyclist.

Chapter 3

Get Training on How to Ride a Motorcycle

Formal training is now required

Motorcycle forums on the Internet have been heating up with
messages about learning how to ride a motorcycle. In 1989, when I
first took up motorcycling, there was little information around
about classes that one might take to learn to ride. The Motorcycle
Safety Foundation (MSF) existed but was not well known. This
was a good six years before most people had even heard of the
Internet. My local Honda motorcycle dealer certainly didn't know
about the MSF. The 800 number was finally found in one of my
motorcycle magazines and arrangements were made to attend the
beginner's class.

Today, with the emergence of the Internet and the existence of
many motorcycle Web sites including my site, Motorcycle Views,
access to information about the MSF is more abundant. New riders
still want to learn how to ride safely. Many of them frequent
Internet motorcycle forums that readily discuss training and the
MSF.

I once received an email from a rider getting back into
motorcycling after a 20 year absence. Excerpts from this email are
given below to show you what real people are doing and thinking
about regarding motorcycle training. After the email are excerpts
from forum threads about MSF courses. Finally, there is a link to
the MSF so you can pursue your own training.

There is a difference of opinion among forum members regarding
their own experiences with MSF training. Some loved it. Some
hated it. Some failed but want to try again. Some got thrown out.
My own experiences were positive but there are elements of a
military operation embedded in the MSF training. It is not easy and

you may get yelled at a lot but the objective is to make you aware of what you are doing wrong on the closed- course range so you won't make as many mistakes on the street. Even after 24 years, my head still rings with the words of my female instructor: "Keep your head up, keep your head up, keep your head up!" The words you hear from your own range instructors may be different but heed them. They will save your life.

Email from js in Arizona:

"Thank you very much for all of the informative articles on motorcycle safety. It has been about 20 years since I've been on a motorcycle and I thought that taking an MSF class would be very beneficial. For the past several weeks I have been reading anything and everything I could find relating to safety, including your tips.

Today I went to pick up my new Honda Shadow VLX. I felt somewhat intimidated by this motorcycle. It was not just the fact that I had not ridden in so long but this is also the biggest bike I have ever owned. I told the salesman that I wanted to get the feel of it before venturing out into traffic.

The engine was purring contentedly as I swung my leg over the bike and strapped on my helmet. The overriding thought going through my mind was, 'take it slow and don't get killed on this thing!' I straightened the bike up and raised the kick stand. Putting it in 1st gear I very gingerly turned the throttle until the rpms increased just slightly while letting out the clutch. The bike began to roll forward and I immediately applied both brakes bringing it to a stop. So far so good, I thought. Now the big test, a left hand turn around a concrete street divider. There was a truck parked in a driveway just past the curve with its flashers on, obviously making a delivery. As I slowly began rolling and just started to make my turn, to my horror I saw his backup lights come on. Hitting both brakes, I came to a quick stop but I had forgotten to pull in the clutch and the bike died, leaning at a precarious angle.

Many of your safety tips came back to me as I was driving home. I am looking forward to taking the MSF class and learning how to 'start' riding a motorcycle the correct way." -- js from Arizona

More about MSF Training

The following excerpts came from forum discussions. They're indicative of what new riders are talking about regarding training.

Passed the Motorcycle Safety Course!

"Whoopee! I just graduated from the MSF beginner's course. The way I see it, what I learned this weekend will probably save my life several times over, and I intend to practice the skills I was taught every chance I get."

What is up with the MSF course?

"After reading Chrisie's post about getting asked to leave the MSF course due to not being able to make circles tight enough, I have to wonder what is up with these guys."

Help -- MSF sold out

"I just called to sign up for my local MSF safety course and...it's sold out thru the end of June, with a waiting list of 10 people per course! So, my question is...what now?"

MSF Course Prices

"The MSF course is $370.00 here, so you would have to tell the 17-year-old young man interested in getting his first ride to add a couple of hundred bucks to the $70.00 he thought he had to pay."

MSF Course

"I would appreciate it if those of you who have participated in a MSF course could address the following: Several folks who have taken the course claimed that they put you through several practices/procedures (braking for one) that can cause you to dump your bike. What do those of you who have attended the course say?"

Motorcycle Safety Course

"This might seem like a pretty ignorant question, but what are the motorcycle safety courses all about? I have seen numerous posts about people taking motorcycle safety courses. So far as I know, the only thing that has changed is that the new licensees have to drive around a bunch of cones in the parking lot."

That Darn MSRC

"I've been wanting to ride since I was 15. I'm 52 and have just bought my first bike. I have taken the MSRC twice and been kicked out both times. When I asked the instructor what I did wrong he said, 'Lots of things. You were too jerky on the throttle and you didn't lean the bike, you just leaned your upper body.' He tried to tell me about counter steering. I admit, I have difficulty with this."

MSF Tragedy

"Last evening we started our MSF course, with a full class load of 12 people. Classroom hours went well, and we were prepared for riding this morning. We started with the 'duck walk,' then buddy push, and so forth and finally, the big moment arrived for almost the entire class of newbies except for one woman who blew out of the track, fixated on a brick garage, and nailed it head-on at about 12 mph, head first."

The Message is Clear

Take an MSF class to learn how to ride a motorcycle. Here's the address of the MSF I promised earlier: www.msf-usa.org. Now, take charge and get trained to be a safe motorcycle rider.

Chapter 4

Motorcycle Types

New riders are often unaware that there are many types of motorcycles. These motorcycle types or styles have evolved from the standard motorcycle.

This article describes 10 motorcycle types. I've illustrated each type with a picture. Some pictures show the owners of the bikes so you can get an idea how you might look on the bike.

No one can tell you what motorcycle type is best for you. That's part of the fun, sitting on bikes and looking at specs to determine what type fits you. The odds are, you will go through most of the types during your riding career. That's just the way it is. What suits you as a beginner looks and feels less appealing later on. My progression so far has been: two standards, three tourers, a trike, and a standard. Your mileage will vary.

Standard Motorcycles

© 2005 Walter Kern

A standard bike is what most new riders see when they take an MSF class. The rider sits pretty much straight up with the foot pegs directly straight down. The angle of the fork -- the rake -- is slight allowing for easy turning of the handlebars and easy balancing of the bike at all speeds.

Shown here is my former 1994 Harley-Davidson Sportster XLH1200. I also owned a Honda CM400T and a Honda Nighthawk CB750, also standards.

There is often some confusion in motorcycle types. What one person calls a standard, another calls a cruiser.

Cruisers

© 2005 Thomas E. Long

Cruisers are normally motorcycles with low seat heights, fat rear tires, raked front forks, and forward controls with the foot pegs way out in front to the point that your rear end takes a lot of the road jolts. With a standard bike, your foot pegs are straight down allowing you to lift yourself off the seat when you see a pothole coming. With the cruiser, you hope the rear suspension will take care of that for you.

Cruisers are great to look at. They handle beautifully at high speeds but their low speed handling can find you on the ground if you happen to be turning the front wheel just as you have to grab a lot of front brake. I dumped my wife's Honda Shadow VLX600 cruiser that way a couple of times. It was on the ground in the blink of an eye.

Most Harley-Davidson motorcycles are cruisers. Honda, Yamaha, Suzuki, and Kawasaki have many cruiser models. In fact, the cruiser type is the most popular motorcycle type.

Shown here is a Harley-Davidson Softail Deuce. As with most Harley cruisers, it was customized a bit for its owner with custom paint, a 1550 Big Bore, Drag Bars with braided cables, back rest and various pieces of chrome added.

Naked Bikes

© 2005 Tracy L. Pursell

A naked bike is basically a standard motorcycle with little wind protection and an exposed chassis. It's an example of a motorcycle you can usually see through.

An example of a naked bike is the one shown here, a Ducati 600 Monster Dark. Others include the Buell Blast, BMW K1200R, Harley-Davidson Sportster, Triumph Speed Triple, Yamaha FZ1 and Yamaha V-Max.

Lately, many publications have been writing about the naked bike and most moto-journalists agree that the naked bike has become a defined motorcycle type.

Sportbikes

© 2005 Vicki Gray

Sportbikes are the flashiest of all motorcycles. They're lightweight, fast, and include colorful paint jobs.

The picture shown here is Vicki Gray, professional racer, who has also appeared on The Learning Channel (TLC) in Biker Girls: Born to Be Wild. She rides a Honda CBR600RR.

Sportbikes are the bad boys of motorcycles. They're pretty to look at and inexpensive to buy, but with the wrong rider aboard, they can become a deadly weapon. Motorists have long complained about sportbikes in packs, racing and darting in and out of traffic. I was personally confronted with a group of about 100 sportbikes that overtook me when I was already going 65 mph. I was passed like I was standing still. Then a single rider pulled up in front of my trike, turned his head around and looked the trike and me over for a about 20 seconds. He then sped off. It was unnerving. Unfortunately, the general public seems to have the same impression of sportbike riders, whether it's true or not.

The speed and acceleration of sportbikes make them very quick in traffic. Since they're fast, a lot of new riders want their first bike to be a sportbike. Resist the temptation.

So, if you want to ride a sportbike, first get trained and practice a lot. Wear protective apparel and be a responsible rider. Then you and your sportbike will be perfect together.

Dual-Sport Motorcycles

© 2003 Glen Smith

Dual-Sports or dual-purpose bikes are universal bikes. For those who want to ride on the street and also not be afraid to take an off-road detour, the dual-sport bike is the perfect choice.

Dual-Sports have tall seat heights, long suspensions, and are street legal. These are not bikes for beginners. Adventure-touring bikes are similar except have added saddlebags, windshields, and other long distance features.

The picture shows a KTM LC4 640 Adventure dual-sport which could also serve as an adventure-touring bike. This bike is right at home on the Las Vegas Strip or the desert trails.

Touring Motorcycles

© 2005 Andre Pahud

Touring Motorcycles are the ultimate long distance motorcycles. They come with the biggest engines, great acceleration and cruising speed, lots of storage including top trunks and saddlebags, amenities like cruise control, stereo radios, CB communications, reverse gears, onboard air compressors, large fairings and windshields, heated seats and grips, and high reliability.

Shown here is a Honda Gold Wing 1500. Honda has most of the market in touring motorcycles. They stopped making the 1500 in 2000 replacing it with the Gold Wing 1800. For 2006, the Gold Wing became available with an onboard navigation system, ABS brakes, and even an integral airbag.

Although it's possible to tour on any type of motorcycle -- and many do -- these touring motorcycles make riding two-up on a 3000 mile trip as comfortable as riding down to the local ice cream store.

Examples of the touring bike are the Honda Gold Wing 1800, BMW K1200LT, Harley-Davidson Ultra Classic Electra Glide, and Yamaha FJR1300AE.

Some bikes with somewhat less amenities plus superior handling characteristics are a cross between a sportbike and a touring bike. They're called Sport-Tourers. Examples are the Honda ST1300, BMW R1100S, and the Ducati ST4s.

Motorcycle Trikes

© 2004 Michael Bergman

Most people would not define trikes as a motorcycle type. However, the growth of trikes is certainly noticeable as more and more riders find themselves unable to ride a two-wheeler anymore or just like the concept of triking over biking. My wife was riding a Honda PC800 but a medical problem prevented her from holding up the bike anymore so I converted my Gold Wing 1500 to a trike for her. I then bought another Gold Wing for myself but liked the trike so much, I decided to convert my new Wing to a trike also.

When I attend the Americade rally, I often hang around the Motor Trike area and listen to reasons why people want trikes. Yes, age and infirmities do seem to be a large part of it. However, there are also people who just want to ride and don't want to start with a 2-wheeler. And there are those whose spouses have complained about being dumped off the back of a bike too many times. They like the concept of a stable trike.

The trike is symmetrical, unlike a sidecar rig. Most are built on Gold Wing platforms so they have a low center of gravity, shaftdrive, reverse gear, and all the creature comforts of the Wing. The picture shown here is a 2003 Honda Gold Wing 1800 w/Lehman Trike Conversion.

These days, other brands are also being converted, notably Harley-Davidson. With half a dozen major trike conversion companies, the market is booming.

Trikes attract a lot of attention. Don't buy one if you like to be left alone.

Motorcycle Classics

© 2005 Steve McLaughlin, Prof

I get to go to a lot of bike gatherings. One of the great side benefits is when I happen upon a classic bike. Now a classic bike can be an old motorcycle or it can just as well be a new bike with a classic or retro style.

The picture, shown here, is of a 1946 Indian Chief Roadmaster that spends its time scooting around Hawaii.

Despite the fact that motorcycles have been around more than 100 years, you just can't go out and find a classic without a lot of work. You need to find a bike that still has parts support. It should also have a devoted legion of followers who have banded together in antique, vintage or classic clubs. Such clubs could be local or just found on the Internet.

Many classics are old Indians. You may even see an old Vincent if you're lucky. Many people look for a bike they once owned in their youth. If you end up having to restore an old machine into a classic, you might want to read about one man's search in the book, "Rebuilding the Indian: A Memoir," by Fred Haefele.

Motor Scooters

© 2005 Jerry & Geneva Nugent

As was the case for trikes, motor scooters are not really a motorcycle type either. They are, however, taking a more prominent place within motorcycling. That's because they get better gas mileage, are simpler to operate, take up less space, are easier to maneuver, and are easier to mount and dismount. Anyone with a leg movement problem who can't flip a leg over a bike anymore, can easily step into a motor scooter and ride off using an automatic transmission.

Motor scooters are step-through or feet-forward vehicles with smaller wheels than motorcycles. They tend to have automatic transmissions. They range in engine size from 50cc to 600cc with the 400-600cc machines most capable of sustained highway speeds and capabilities to keep up with regular motorcycles.

Many riders had a motor scooter for their first 2-wheeled vehicle. When I was growing up, the rage was the Cushman motor scooter. These days, the metropolitan areas seem to be a magnet for machines such as the Vespa. For those already experienced in riding motorcycles, some new motor scooter riders are buying Suzuki Burgman 400 and 650 machines or Honda Silver Wing 600 scooters. Honda also has a line of scooters ranging from the 50cc Ruckus up to the Silver Wing.

Shown here is a Suzuki Burgman AN650 motor scooter.

Motorcycle Choppers and Customs

© 2005 Allan Le Beau

Choppers are motorcycles that have had certain components "chopped off." That was the original definition when returning soldiers looked at the bikes on the market and decided that they needed to be lighter, more streamlined, have more performance, and be as utilitarian as possible They also wanted their bikes to reflect their personalities and often make a statement of their philosophy of life. So they began to take components off and modify the rest. They wanted to have a chopper.

Choppers tended to be creations executed by their owners. In recent years, motorcycle companies have been formed to create mass produced choppers. Large companies such as Big Dog (now out of business, a victim of the 2011 economy), to small companies such as Wicked Women Choppers, have been formed to satisfy the growing market.

Custom motorcycles may look similar to choppers or they may be complete customizations of an existing bike, or ground-up builds of new designs using off-the-shelf and custom made parts. It's sometimes possible to get a custom from a regular manufacturer but most come from shops being paid to take an owner's ideas and create a unique bike to fit him or her only. National TV shows such as The Discovery Channel's Biker Build-Off series and the American Chopper series have brought a whole new audience to the love of choppers and customs.

Chapter 5

Basic Gear for a Motorcycle Beginner

Beginning riders often have no clue as to what else they need to buy after they have purchased their first motorcycle. It turns out that the list of motorcycle gear is quite long.

Here is some essential motorcycle gear that you need to have with you as you ride.

Lots more can be added later as you increase the size of your bike. Of course you still need to find places to store all the extra motorcycle gear. That's why people end up with big touring bikes pulling trailers or rat bikes piled high with junk festooned with multiple interlocking bungee nets.

Legal Stuff

Please satisfy all legal requirements to become a motorcyclist, including obtaining your motorcycle driver's license.

I recommend that you take a Motorcycle Safety Foundation Course (MSF). Many of these courses provide an automatic endorsement on your existing automobile license upon completion. Otherwise, satisfy the governmental requirements to obtain your license.

Get motorcycle insurance to protect yourself and others you may come in contact with on the road.

Clothing

Get a DOT approved helmet. Helmets are very controversial among experienced riders. Some don't want the government requiring them to be worn. Take my advice, while you are learning, always wear a helmet. I prefer a full-face helmet and never go anywhere without one. It's also great for keeping the bugs out of your teeth and the rain out of your eyes.

Buy a leather motorcycle jacket. Don't buy just any leather jacket. Motorcycle jackets are not normally sold in regular stores. Check out local motorcycle dealers, the motorcycle magazines, and the Internet. Get a good quality jacket with vents front and back that will allow air to circulate in the summer. Brands like Hein Gericke, Aerostich, Joe Rocket, and Roadgear come to mind. In recent years, many riders are switching to lighter weight textile jackets with padding in strategic areas. These are great and I have one myself but the leather jacket, although heavier and hotter, still protects the best.

Wear jeans. It goes without saying that most riders wear jeans. Some may want armored jeans for more protection. Those you see wearing shorts, T-shirts, and sneakers are not to be emulated unless you like sliding your skin across the asphalt at 60mph.

Riding pants should be considered. Your best bet is a pair of heavy leather chaps or leather pants. The chaps are nice because they are easy to put on over your jeans and remove when you get to your destination.

Don't ride without leather gloves. Select a lightweight pair for summer and a heavy pair for cold weather riding.

I prefer to wear full length leather boots with no laces. Laces can easily cause your foot to be immobilized just as you want to put it down to stop. Be sure that the boots have rubber soles and heels to grip the road when you stop.

Wear long socks that extend higher than the boots and won't ride down.

Get a rain suit. These come in one-piece and two-piece versions. Both will keep you dry when it rains. If you do any serious riding, you will encounter rain. Be prepared. Often just the presence of a rain suit in your saddlebags will keep the rain from falling.

Riding suits can wait till later. They can be expensive unless money is no object.

A leather triangle that fits around your neck will protect it and eliminate drafts.

A balaclava, a silk-thin head cover, can be worn to keep you warm during winter rides.

Survival Equipment

Roadside Assistance Plan: Maybe your plan is to call a family member to bring a trailer. Better yet is a national plan such as provided by Towbusters or MTS that will come to you and tow you to the nearest dealer or repair facility.

Cellphone: I carry one in my pocket. Get one and find a place on the bike to carry it.

Flat Kit: Usually contains various plugs and procedures to implant them in nail holes. It's good to have a CO_2 cylinder or onboard air compressor to pump up the tire.

First Aid Kit: I've saved quite a few riders with just a Band-Aid out of my billfold. A complete first aid kit is better.

Water Bottle: On hot rides, you'll need this one. It can also help when you need water to wash your windshield.

Reflective Vest: This is highly visible and helps others to see you, especially at night.

Ear Plugs: Most riders develop hearing problems especially if they ride with no windshield and a minimal helmet. Ear plugs are cheap, easy to use, and will save your hearing.

Heated Clothing: If you expect to ride in the winter or at high altitude, you must be prepared for cold temperatures. I always carry an electric vest and electric gloves that are connected to the battery through an adjustable temperature control. I've seen some riders stuff newspapers in their jackets and jeans or get out their rain suits to ward off the cold temperatures.

Tools

Owner's Manual: Get a detailed owner's manual or shop manual for your bike and see what types of tools are recommended for your model. If the bike comes with a tool kit, examine it and determine if you need more tools. At any rate, always take the toolkit with you on the bike. Here are some essential tools.

Screwdrivers: You'll need assorted regular and Phillips screwdrivers.

Pliers: You should have regular pliers, small ViseGrip pliers, and needlenose pliers.

Wrenches: Get Allen, Torx, sparkplug, open-end, adjustable, and combination in sizes needed for your model.

Loctite: Keeps fasteners from loosening or falling off.

Miscellaneous Stuff

Kickstand Plate: Don't put your sidestand down in hot asphalt or grass. Use a thin metal plate, beer can, or other plate for protection.

Bungee Cords and Nets: These can help you carry almost anything on your bike. Ratbikes are loaded with them.

Helmet Extender: This is a 3-4 inch extender that slips through the ring of your helmet and attaches to your regular helmet locking device. If you don't have any locking device on your bike, you may have to carry your helmet with you when you park.

Bike Cover: There are some very small covers that fit the windshield and pull over the bike to cover the seat. Of course, there are also full body covers that can be difficult to get back in that small carrying bag.

Tire Gauge: Don't ride without checking the pressure in your tires. Be sure to read the pressure when your tires are cold.

Swiss Army Knife: They contain everything from cork screws to screwdrivers with even a knife blade or two thrown in.

Small Flashlight: This is a must after dark. Keep it where you can find it without using it first.

Duct Tape: Absolute necessity.

Electrical Tape: Just a small amount will come in handy someday.

Rags: Use for washing your windshield if nothing else.

Accessories

Windshield: It may spoil the looks of your bike but on a trip of any length, it will keep you from tiring out. It's also a must for winter riding.

Saddlebags: Where else are you going to put all this stuff? You may find that you need a top trunk or even a travel trailer as you get more into motorcycling.

Chapter 6

Ten Ways to Be Safe on a Motorcycle

1. Assume Drivers Can't See You: Ride assuming that you and your motorcycle are totally invisible to motorists. That means you must never assume that drivers can see you. The odds are, they can't so believe it yourself and always have an "out" for dangerous traffic situations. Motorcycle Safety depends on you.

2. Maintain Safe Spacing: Leave plenty of space in front and back and to the sides from all other vehicles. Be an island. Stay away from traffic as much as possible. This gives you more visibility and more time to react to situations.

3. Anticipate Trouble: Anticipate trouble situations and know what to do when you see them. Analyze what vehicles are doing and try to predict the outcome. Then make sure you're ready to avoid a bad traffic situation.

4. Beware of Oncoming Left Turners: Beware of oncoming motorists turning left in front of you at intersections. This is the leading cause of death of motorcycle riders. I'm deadly serious here. I have personally lost many friends to this accident. If you only remember one tip here, let it be this one. Slow down before you enter an intersection. Have an escape route planned. Stay visible. Don't travel too close to cars in front of you. Position your bike so it can be seen by the left turner. Eye contact is not enough.

5. Ride Your Own Ride: Don't try to keep up with your friends who may be more experienced. Know your personal limits. Ride your own ride.

6. Watch Out for Curves: Beware of taking curves that you can't see around. A parked truck or a patch of sand may be awaiting you.

7. Don't Give In to Road Rage: Do not give in to road rage and try to "get even" with another rider or motorist. If you follow these tips, most likely you won't fall victim to road rage. It's better to calm down, slow down, and collect your thoughts first. Then continue on and enjoy the ride. That's what we're all out there for in the first place.

8. Don't allow Tailgating: If someone is tailgating you, either speed up to open more space or pull over and let them pass. Life is too short. Remember that a bike can stop faster than a car so you don't want a truck on your tail when you find yourself trying to brake to avoid an accident. Also, don't tailgate the vehicle in front of you. Oncoming drivers can't see you.

9. Don't Be Blinded by Sun Glare: Beware of riding your motorcycle into sun glare. All it takes is turning a corner and finding the sun either directly in your face or passing straight through your windshield. Some helmets have shields to block the sun. Face shields help somewhat. But sometimes you just find yourself blinded by the light. Slow down, pull over, shield your eyes and look for a way to change direction.

10. Avoid Riding at Night: Avoid riding at night, especially late Saturday night and early Sunday when drunken drivers may be on the road. It goes without saying that you shouldn't drink and ride. Going bar hopping? Leave the bike at home and find a designated driver.

What Am I Trying To Say About Motorcycle Safety?

The best way to be safe is to take a Motorcycle Safety Foundation (MSF) course to learn the basic ways to control your motorcycle and to learn how to recognize traffic situations that you need to be ready to handle.

Always wear protective clothing and a helmet. A tiny beanie helmet held on by a thin strap and affixed with a fake DOT sticker is not enough.

Maintain your bike so it is safe too. Keep records of the intervals when you replace tires, chains, clutch cables, batteries, brakes, etc. You don't want an equipment malfunction to contribute to a motorcycle accident.

Practice riding under all kinds of traffic situations. Ride with a buddy if at all possible. Avoid riding long distances alone.

Become a member of a motorcycle forum or social network that caters to motorcyclists and read what other experienced riders have to say about how to ride safely.

I want you to become an aged motorcyclist because you know how to survive on a motorcycle. I don't want to read about you in the newspaper or on a motorcycle forum or mailing list as yet another motorcycle statistic. Learn how to be safe and responsible on a motorcycle. That's why my Website, Motorcycle Views, exists and that's why I'm writing these tips. The rest is up to you.

Ride Safe

Chapter 7

How to Get Back Into Riding Motorcycles Again

Many riders are coming back into motorcycling after a long absence, some as long as 30 years or more. These are riders who reached a point in their lives where family obligations or their economic situation forced them to sell their motorcycle or put it into storage. As the years passed, their situations changed and the love of riding came back with a vengeance. However, motorcycles have changed, training methods have changed, and motorcycle safety has become a priority.

Are you one of these returning motorcycle riders? Here's what you need to know to do it right the second time around.

Things Have Changed

If you haven't been keeping up with the progress in motorcycling since you gave up the sport years ago, you may be in for a surprise. There are a wide variety of both domestic and foreign bikes available that are cool to look at and much more fun to ride. Models run the gamut from scooters to cruisers, to standards, to sportbikes, to dual sports, to touring bikes, and even to trikes.

Motorcycle trikes are relatively new to the sport even though they existed more than 40 years ago. New trikes are extremely stable and possess riding characteristics unheard of until recently. Some returning riders choose trikes to deal with various infirmities.

You'll also find a change in motorcycle riding apparel and helmets. Various synthetic materials are now being used, as well as leather for jackets. Helmet use is now controlled by law in some areas. Check local regulations.

Learning how to ride a motorcycle is now much more organized with numerous classes available.

With the popularity of the Internet, there are now thousands of motorcycle resources available that allow you to stay current with what's going on in motorcycling. For example, many people become regulars on one or more motorcycle forums. These forums can attract thousands of visitors daily. If you have any question about motorcycling, you can post it on the forum and get immediate responses from all over the world by numerous experts. Social networks such as Facebook, Twitter, and Google+ are also attracting many riders into Internet groups.

Get Trained to Ride a Motorcycle

I cannot emphasize this enough: You must take a formal motorcycle training course from a school that uses the Motorcycle Safety Foundation (MSF) methods. You may think you already know how to ride a motorcycle but attending one of these courses will give you the latest skills required to be a safe rider. These courses are usually given over a weekend with both classroom instruction and field exercises. Motorcycles are provided. The classes teach you how to ride the machine, but more importantly, they teach you street survival skills.

If you feel you are already an experienced motorcycle rider, you may want to enroll in an MSF experienced rider course. These courses are conducted with you riding your own motorcycle.

Get a Bike

I don't recommend going down to your local motorcycle dealer and buying a new motorcycle. Perhaps you've known someone who decided to get back into motorcycling and the first thing they did was buy a big heavyweight machine. Now, it's possible that some people who have natural athletic abilities may be able to pull this off. The vast majority, however, will not be able to do it. They will end up damaging the bike numerous times and most likely injuring themselves in the bargain.

You want to start off with a simple, cheap, standard motorcycle and be prepared to see it fall over a few times while you get used to riding again. You should be able to find something for $1000 or less. Just be sure that the bike runs well, has good tires and brakes, and that you insure it.

At some point, if you haven't maintained the motorcycle endorsement on your driver's license, you'll have to take a motorcycle road test offered by the Dept. of Motor Vehicles for your state or other governmental authority. A possible side benefit of taking the MSF beginner's course is an automatic endorsement without having to take the normal motorcycle vehicle tests. Check your local regulations.

Practice and Become Proficient Riding a Motorcycle

Before you venture out to get in some serious motorcycle riding practice, be sure to first buy protective apparel. Then you'll need to scout your buddies for a riding partner. Your goal now is to improve the skills you learned in the MSF course by actual street riding. As you become proficient, you may have the urge to begin helping other riders and even want to share your experiences with the world. Here's how.

Buy Protective Clothing

Clothing is for comfort, protection, and safety. The first thing you have to protect is your head. I recommend that you wear a helmet at least for the first year while you're bringing up your skill level.

You should wear gloves specially made for riding. If you fall and hit the road, most likely, your hands will hit first. Let the road rash be on your gloves, not your hands.

You should wear full-length motorcycle boots with rubber soles and heels. Boots limit foot and leg injuries should you fall. They also give you a bit more height to allow your feet to touch the ground when you're stopped.

I prefer a leather jacket with vents. During the summer, I open the vents to allow air circulation. During the winter, I put in a liner to retain body heat. Riding in the summer in 90 degree heat without a jacket will dry your skin quickly. A jacket will retain skin moisture and cool you. If you go down, you will thank the day you decided to wear leather. Leather pants or chaps are great if you want further protection. Many riders like full riding suits either of leather or synthetic material.

The reality is that riders will ride with almost anything on, sometimes offering practically no protection at all. It's your call but I hope you'll think about what I've recommended here and make an informed decision.

Get a Buddy and Practice

Find an experienced motorcyclist -- preferably one who has received MSF training -- to go out with you and act as your mentor for a couple of months. Ride around in your local area first avoiding busy roads and heavy traffic. Gradually ride on the country roads, the highways, and then the high-speed roads as you gain experience. Try to be aware of all you learned in your MSF training and put it into practice.

After six months to a year, you'll be ready for a better bike, maybe a new one.

Be an Example

As a returning rider, you know the basics. However, since things have changed so much, you will find yourself learning lots of new things and ways of thinking. You'll find that safety is a much bigger thing than it used to be. You'll see that many more women are now riding motorcycles. Often, the MSF classes contain more women than men.

As an older rider, you'll be an instant role model for others who have also been thinking about getting back into riding again. You may find yourself the local expert in how to do that. So prepare yourself to reenter motorcycling but be ready to start assisting others who see how much fun you're having.

Share Your Experiences

As you start checking off the steps outlined here, make yourself known to the members of a motorcycle forum or social network where you feel most comfortable. Many of them have been where you are now and can help you. In addition, your problems will help others to anticipate potential problems they may have. The result is a sort of town meeting of motorcyclists all helping one another to become better and safer riders.

You can be a motorcyclist again, except this time you will be a better and safer rider and you'll be riding a fantastic modern motorcycle.

Chapter 8

Seven Things Only a Biker Knows

The following is certainly nothing new for an experienced motorcyclist. However, people brand new to motorcycling and those who are on the outside of motorcycling, will find that bikes are quite different from cars.

We are assuming modern motorcycles and cars driven on the right side of the road. These items do not apply completely to motor scooters.

Over the last 100+ years of motorcycle history, there have been many configurations of motorcycle controls. Fortunately, standardization did occur and now you can go from one bike to another and be able to ride it safely.

1. You Shift Gears with Your Left Foot

Most cars have automatic transmissions these days. Manual transmission cars do exist. You use your right hand to shift a car. Bikes are different. You shift gears by kicking a ratchet down smartly for each lower gear. The normal configuration is 1-N-2-3-4-5-6, assuming a 6-speed transmission. N stands for Neutral. If your bike is in first gear, you go to second gear by kicking upward smartly with the toe of your boot on the bottom of the shifter. A similar action is done to go through the remaining gears one at a time. I won't go into all the operations required to support the shift such as use of the clutch.

2. The Clutch Lever is on the Left Handlebar Grip

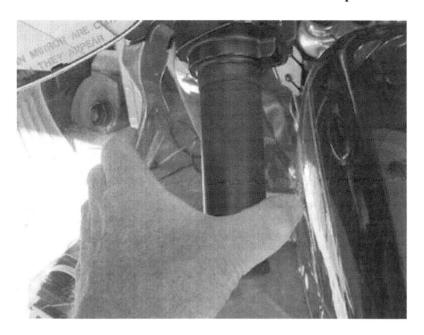

For those used to driving a car with a manual transmission, the clutch is on the floor just to the left of the brake pedal. On a motorcycle, the clutch lever -- no pedal -- is squeezed by the fingers of the left hand. Squeeze the lever until it is close to the left handlebar grip to activate the clutch. Release your grip gradually and apply a bit of throttle just after you have shifted gears and the bike will be moving in another gear.

The motorcycle clutch lever is either connected to a cable that goes to the physical clutch release mechanism or it is hydraulically operated. Use of a hydraulic clutch eliminates broken clutch cables and makes using the clutch easier.

3. The Front Brake Lever is on the Right Handlebar Grip

In a car, there is a single brake pedal that controls the brakes on all four wheels. On a motorcycle, there are various braking systems in use that separately control the brakes on the front wheel and the brakes on the rear wheel. To control the brakes, a motorcycle has a front wheel brake lever located on the right handlebar grip and a rear wheel brake pedal. Modern bikes have disc brakes on the front wheel and either disc or drum brakes on the rear wheel.

The front brake is the most important brake on the motorcycle. It has about 70-80 percent of the total stopping force. On a motorcycle, riders use the two brakes together but favor the front brake in most situations. Beginning riders without training often use the rear brake and avoid the front brake. The result is a significantly increased distance to get the bike stopped.

Some bikes have Linked Braking Systems (LBS) where squeezing the front brake lever activates a portion of the front braking action and also activates a portion of the braking action on the rear disc brake. (Some examples are the Honda Gold Wing 1800 and Honda ST1300.) The Honda Gold Wing 1500 has a Unified Braking System (UBS) where the front brake lever controls the right front disc brake only while depressing the rear brake pedal applies the left front disc brake as well as the rear disc brake. Also, optional ABS brakes are used on bikes, as in cars, to stop the bike without locking the wheels on slick surfaces.

4. The Rear Brake is Controlled by the Right Foot

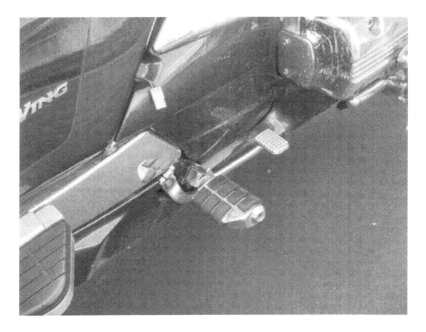

In a car, there is a single brake pedal that controls the brakes on all four wheels. On a motorcycle, there are various braking systems in use that separately control the brakes on the front wheel and the brakes on the rear wheel. To do this, a motorcycle has a front wheel brake lever and a rear wheel brake pedal.

The rear wheel brake on a motorcycle can be either disc or drum with most modern bikes using disc brakes. The rear wheel brake has its own master cylinder and associated foot pedal on the right side of the bike. Of all the controls used to operate a motorcycle, the rear wheel brake, controlled by a brake pedal on the right side of the bike, is most like the brake pedal on a car. For that reason, many beginning riders tend to favor the brake pedal thinking that it is all that is required to stop the motorcycle. Such is not the case since the front brake is the most important on the motorcycle. It has about 70-80 percent of the total stopping force. On a motorcycle, riders use the two brakes together but favor the front brake in most situations. Beginning riders without training often use the rear brake and avoid the front brake. The result is a significantly increased distance to get the bike stopped.

Bikes also may have systems where depressing the rear foot brake also activates a portion of the braking action on the front wheel. Also, optional ABS brakes are used on bikes, as in cars, to stop the bike without locking the wheels on slick surfaces.

5. The Throttle is Controlled by Twisting the Right Handlebar Grip

In a car, the speed is controlled by the accelerator pedal. The harder you push your foot down on the accelerator, the faster the car goes. Release the pedal and the speed decreases. On a motorcycle, the speed is controlled by the throttle that is built-in to the right handlebar grip. Twist the grip toward you and the speed increases. Relax your grip and the speed decreases.

There's a lot of action on the right handlebar grip and considerable coordination is required. The right hand must be continually adjusting the speed up and down while also activating the front brake. Also, when turning the bike, the rider must press the right handlebar grip forward to make the bike turn right or possibly pull the right grip backwards to make the bike turn left. Also, some bikes have turn signal switches on each handlebar grip so one might have to press a switch to indicate that a right turn was anticipated and press it again when the turn is completed.

6. A Bike Has a KILL Switch

Cars don't have KILL switches. The closest you can come is to turn off the ignition. On a motorcycle, a KILL switch has several purposes.

The motorcycle KILL (or STOP) switch is in series with the ignition switch. When the KILL switch is open, the motorcycle will not start.

Most motorcycle training courses suggest that you get in the habit of using the motorcycle KILL switch to shut off your bike. The reasoning is that if you don't use it, it won't work when you need to use it.

Much confusion occurs in traffic when you inadvertently trip the KILL switch and then can't figure out why the bike won't restart. Always look at the KILL switch first.

You may need to use the KILL switch if your bike falls over and you can't reach the ignition. Just trip the KILL switch. KILL switches are also known as RUN or STOP switches.

7. You Turn a Bike by Countersteering

Cars turn by turning a steering wheel. A bike has handlebars and turns not by steering but countersteering.

At all but parking lot speeds, a motorcycle turns by pressing the right handlebar grip forward to turn right and pushing the left handlebar grip forward to turn left. In other words: push right, go right; push left, go left. This is countersteering.

To confuse matters even more, a trike or sidecar rig (3-wheels) does not countersteer. It steers just like a car. Push right - go left; push left - go right. That's because these three-wheelers don't lean as motorcycles do.

Motorcycles turn by leaning. There are various ways to get the bike to lean and there are various experts who claim their way is the best. Countersteering is the fastest way to get the bike to lean. Pressing the right grip forward, turns the wheel to the left moving the contact patch to the left. The bike is then pulled over to the right into a right lean, thereby initiating a right turn. Don't believe it? Stand in front of a bike as it approaches you at speed and have the rider push the right grip forward. You will see a momentary wheel-turn to the left quickly followed by a lean to the right and a turn to the right.

Are There More than Seven?

There are obviously more than Seven Things Only a Biker Knows. Continue reading this book and learn many more or visit my Motorcycle Views Website.

Chapter 9

Ten Motorcycle Myths

There are many motorcycle myths out there. Here is my list of motorcycle myths.

1. Any group of riders is part of the Hell's Angels.

People on the street seeing bikes go by and not familiar with the world of motorcycling, can sometimes be heard to say, "There goes a bunch of Hell's Angels." I've heard this many times.

We offer no disrespect to the members of the Hell's Angels by reporting this. Perhaps, in some small way, we don't mind being compared with the Hell's Angels. We may have a rebellious spirit. We may like the freedom of riding and the camaraderie of other riders. But most of us either ride alone or with small clubs of like-minded individuals. We have no innate desire to separate ourselves into a lifestyle that may ultimately bring us face-to-face with a disrespect for our own society.

The group shown here is a group of Polar Bear Grand Tour riders just about to arrive at the destination point and sign-in for one of their weekly winter runs, Lewes, DE. I happen to be a member of this organization of 500+ riders.

The terms "rider," "biker," and "motorcyclist" are thrown around a lot these days. The media almost always uses the term "biker." I prefer "motorcyclist." If in doubt, use "rider" as I did in the title to this section.

2. It's better to lay a motorcycle down if you predict an impending crash.

More than 30 years ago, before I even had an interest in motorcycling, I remember hearing talk among co-workers about what they would do if they were riding their bikes and saw an impending crash coming. They all agreed that the best thing to do was to deliberately lay their motorcycles down on the ground to avoid the crash. Some had even practiced doing this.

I didn't know anything about bikes then except that I had always wanted to ride since I was a kid but never did. I thought that this seemed like a strange way to avoid a crash by becoming a crash yourself.

Perhaps this was in the days when tires weren't so sticky and brakes were drum only. I do know that the helmets weren't all that great and that many states didn't have helmet laws. So, it seems even more dangerous now as I think about it than it seemed then when I knew nothing about riding.

Today, the bikes stop faster, some even have ABS brakes to stop in a straight line on any surface.

The helmets are better, the apparel is better. The training is better and people aren't afraid to use their front brakes to stop faster.

So, be prepared with MSF training. Practice good braking techniques. Learn to avoid or swerve around problems and anticipate situations that may force you to react to save your life. Stay on your bike in an upright position. Don't lay your bike down and hope that it will slow you down. It may just flip you into traffic and make things much worse.

Be safe. You may now want to go back and re-read Chapter 6, Ten Ways to Be Safe on a Motorcycle.

3. Bikers wear black leather because they want to look cool.

When you observe motorcyclists in groups, you'll soon become aware that black is the most prominent color: Black leather jackets, black gloves, black boots, black pants, black chaps, even a lot of black motorcycles.

Sure, black leather looks cool. There have even been a few fashion trends recently that featured black everything -- that motorcycle look. However, no rider wears black leather to look cool. Well, maybe a few do but we call them wannabes or poseurs.

Leather is the best protective covering for a rider. It usually comes in black. When you're riding at 65 mph just inches above the ground, you want something on that will keep the pavement away from your skin should you happen to become separated from the machine and hit the ground.

These days, other materials than leather are also being used such as synthetic jackets and pants. These have built-in armor in elbows, shoulders, and back. They are lighter and cool better in hot weather. There are more color choices now but black is still the most prominent color.

Black is not a cool color to be wearing after dark. You can't see it! The newer synthetic jackets are now coming with multiple reflective patches that make you highly visible at night.

This picture is of my wife and me at one of our first rallies. I'm not wearing much leather these days but I am still wearing lots of black.

4. You will eventually get hurt or killed on a motorcycle.

If you don't come from a motorcycle family and decide that you want to learn to ride a motorcycle, usually you get lots of advice from your family. They will tell you, "Motorcycles are dangerous." They'll call them murder-cycles or donor-cycles. They'll remind you that, "Uncle Ed got killed on a motorcycle. You stay away from motorcycles. You'll get killed too."

Now a certain amount of caution is OK so long as it's constructive. They fail to mention that there are many old riders on the road who have been riding 35-60 years and are still alive.

They don't know about all the advances in safety in the last 20 years. Bikes now have disc brakes. Some even have ABS brakes. Most riders are getting trained to ride safely through the programs of the Motorcycle Safety Foundation (MSF).

There are support groups for riders such as motorcycle forums and social networks.

If you come from a motorcycle family, you're still not home free. They will encourage you to ride but they may give you bad advice or worse yet, try to teach you to ride. Don't ever let a loved one teach you to ride. Worst of all is learning totally on your own.

Take my advice. Level the odds by learning all you can about the proper way to ride a motorcycle. Let the MSF teach you. Then get an experienced trusted friend who is also MSF trained to go out with you as you practice. Wear protective apparel and a helmet. You CAN learn to be a safe rider and manage the risks of riding.

5. Harley-Davidson motorcycles leak oil and break down a lot.

This picture was taken at a Polar Bear Grand Tour Christmas Toy Run. It shows a group of 14 Harleys that all came in together and parked together in this corner of the parking lot. Surprisingly, none of them leaked any oil at all and they all started right up after the group returned to their bikes.

The Polar Bear Grand Tour is conducted during the winter months in the NJ-NY-PA-DE region and consists of over 500 riders who brave the weather each Sunday for 22-24 straight weeks. I would say that over 60 percent of these riders are on Harleys and I can't remember the last time I saw one parked on the side of the road during a run, unless he/she was waiting for a buddy to come along.

Tales of leaking and breakdowns tend to relate to bikes of the AMF era between 1969-1981. That was more than 35 years ago. And I'm sure I'll hear from owners of many of these AMF bikes that they haven't had any problems at all.

So, if you've been waiting for Harley to come out with a machine that's reliable and doesn't leak oil, you've been missing a lot of fun. Go check out the complete Harley-Davidson lineup at your local dealer.

6. You should buy your dream bike for your first bike.

When the motorcycle bug bites, it can cause you to be less logical in your thinking. You become obsessed with learning to ride, getting a bike, and finding correct riding apparel.

You start looking at all the new bikes out there and you quickly fall in love with your dream bike. Usually, the bike is way more than you can handle as a beginner.

There is always a steady stream of newbies into motorcycle forums for beginners. It seems that the biggest riders are the ones who claim that they will have no trouble with a big bike. They are strong enough to hold it up -- whatever that means.

The point is that a beginner needs to keep their eye on the goal: Learn how to ride by taking an MSF course and then get a small used learner bike (I bought this 1981 Honda CM400T) for six months to a year to practice riding skills. During this time a new rider will probably drop the bike several times, most in low speed or parking lot situations. These drops won't do much damage to the rider but could cause significant damage to plastic panels on the bike. A new bike will suffer the most damage cost.

Dream bikes may also have too much power for a newbie. A simple momentary twist of the wrist going over a bump could cause a new bike to speed out of control or cross into an opposing lane of traffic too quickly for a newbie to respond.

So, as painful as it is, forego the dream bike for a while until you become proficient in as many street skills as you can. You'll be happy you did.

7. Marlon Brando rode a Harley in the movie, *The Wild One*.

The 1953 movie, *The Wild One*, starring Marlon Brando and Lee Marvin, tells a story of two rival motorcycle gangs as they terrorize a small town after one of their leaders is thrown in jail. Brando and the rest of the Black Rebels Motorcycle Club ride Triumphs and other British motorcycles. In fact, Brando rode his own personal bike, a Triumph Thunderbird 650 in the starring role as Johnny Strabler.

It's a myth that Brando rode a Harley in the movie. It is true that the rival gang, led by Lee Marvin's character, Chino, rode Harley-Davidson motorcycles.

The Wild One was loosely based on the Hollister, California Incident that occurred in 1947 and was reported in Life Magazine.

More information about the movie may be obtained at the IMDb Web site.

Photo courtesy of iBaller.com

8. Motorcycles are only good for short trips and commuting

This seems to be deeply ingrained in the minds of the general public. Whenever I talk to neighbors or strangers while on my bike, they invariably ask, "How far have you been on it?" When I reply that I've ridden cross-country to Yellowstone National Park from New Jersey (see picture), they seem quite surprised.

I got the same reaction when I rode to Indiana for a Gold Wing rally, then home to Illinois for a visit, followed by a return trip through Kentucky, Tennessee, and North Carolina to attend our forum rally at Maggie Valley, and a final trip back to New Jersey. That trip was over 3000 miles, took 17 days, and involved a few skirmishes with the hurricanes that ravaged the USA in late 2005 including Dennis.

Motorcycles don't look like they would take you long distances. There isn't much room to take luggage. Many riders go two-up and that further decreases storage space. Traveling long distances on a motorcycle is called touring.

The fact is that anyone can travel almost anywhere on any kind of motorcycle. Bill Stermer in his book, *Motorcycle Touring and Travel*, states, "The bike on which most people choose to tour tends to be the one they own at the time."

With the increase in reliability of bikes, taking a long tour is nothing special. Bikes have low maintenance engines, shaft drives, adjustable suspensions, fairings, windscreens, and luxury items like stereos, CBs, and cruise control. Most bikes now pull trailers too.

Forget about short trips. Go touring.

9. Never Use the Front Brake Unless You're an Expert Rider

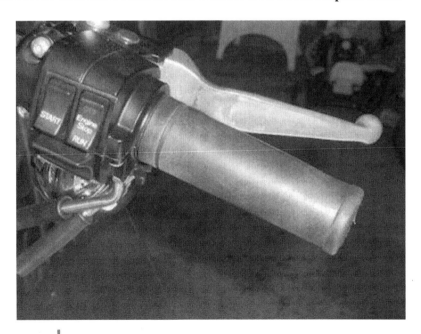

Beginning riders are taught in the Motorcycle Safety Foundation (MSF) courses that effective braking is accomplished by using both front and rear brakes together. There is nothing to fear in using the front brake.

Most modern motorcycles have rear disc brakes. These brakes stop faster, wear longer, and won't fade as much. The rear disc brakes are controlled by the brake pedal.

Beginners often rely only on the rear brake since they can easily activate it using their right foot. Many have been erroneously taught that the front brake, activated by the right hand brake lever (shown here), is to be avoided. However, remember that more than 70 percent of the stopping power of a bike is in the front brake. Get used to using the front brake and the rear brake together. As you progress in your training, you will learn how to use both the front and rear brakes to make fast controlled stops. There are also special situations where different uses of the front and rear brakes are required. When you attend the MSF classes, these situations will be covered.

Since many beginners use the rear brake too much, they often lock them up during panic situations and skid the rear tire. Remember that if you find yourself in a rear wheel skid, DO NOT release the brake pedal. Ride it out. Releasing the pedal will often cause a high side incident. This is the opposite of the advice given for a front-wheel skid with the front brake locked up (release the front brake).

10. BMW Only Makes Cars

Everyone has heard of Harley-Davidson. Maybe that's because they've been making motorcycles since 1903. However, there are other old motorcycle companies that few people know about.

Whenever I stop my motorcycle, I seem to get into conversations about motorcycles with people just walking by. Many times, they'll say, "I used to ride an old Harley but gave it up when I got married." Sometimes people don't know what kind of bike you're riding. Often they guess and say, "Is that a Harley?" Of course, most Japanese cruisers do look a lot like Harleys and even sound like them so it's confusing.

Many times I talk about how I got into riding. My brother-in-law was into BMWs and I was exposed to them when I visited him. The next question is usually, "I thought we were talking about motorcycles. What's a BMW got to do with it." Then I realize that they don't know that BMW also makes motorcycles.

The fact is that BMW made the R32 model in 1923. They hadn't even thought about making cars yet. That didn't happen until 1928 with the Dixi model. The first "real" BMW car, the AM 4, was produced completely in-house in 1932.

The first BMW R32 motorcycle used a flat-twin engine quite similar to the engines used by BMW for the next 75 years.

BMW motorcycles are referred to as Beemers. BMW cars are called Bimmers.

Although BMW only has about 3-4 percent of the motorcycle market, all riders are familiar with BMW and many are devoted to the brand, as shown in the picture.

Are There More than Ten Motorcycle Myths?

Of course there are. I've seen several other similar lists of motorcycle myths. Motorcycle myths are just part of the territory. Unless you become a motorcyclist, you'll never know what motorcycling is all about. It will continue to be one myth after another, a closed society to you. So, be a part of the reality of motorcycling. No more myths for you.

Chapter 10

Buy a Motorcycle

I get a lot of email asking me for advice on the best way to buy a motorcycle. How do you negotiate with dealers? Is the process just like buying a car? What about borrowing money to pay for it? What should you expect to get as a trade-in value when you buy a motorcycle?

Consumer Reports has a yearly issue of its magazine devoted to rating the new cars and giving all kinds of advice on how to get the best deal. There doesn't seem to be anything out there that tells you all aspects of how to buy a motorcycle. So what's a guy or gal supposed to do?

New riders should always start out with a used motorcycle until they get trained and get plenty of practice spread over perhaps a year. New riders tend to take a few spills early on. Damaging a new bike may run into thousands of dollars in repairs, not something that will instill confidence in a rider just starting out while they are trying to develop their skills.

What are your choices? Used or New

Buy a Used Motorcycle

Buy from an auction: Buying a motorcycle from an Internet Auction is the newest way to buy. Two of the most popular services are eBay Motors and Yahoo Auctions.

Buy from a classified ad: Every newspaper has motorcycle want ads. You probably won't have far to travel to see the bike. It will be easy to have a local mechanic check out the bike before you buy it. In addition, there are many Web sites that offer free want ads for motorcycles. You can also check out the classifieds on the various motorcycle forums.

Buy from a friend or acquaintance: Always tell your friends that you are looking to buy a motorcycle. Someone may know someone else who has a bike for sale. If you belong to a motorcycle club or group, announce at a membership gathering that you are looking for another bike. If there is a group newsletter, look for motorcycle ads there. Since any bike you might buy from a group member will probably be well known to you, you don't have to worry as much about the condition of the bike.

Buy from a dealer: You're probably going to be visiting your local dealer anyway. Look for trade-ins in good condition. Why not mention to the salespeople that you are looking for a certain kind of motorcycle to buy. They may work to find a bike for you if they don't have one on the floor.

Buy a New Motorcycle

Buy from the Internet

It's a good thing to use the Internet to do research when you want to buy a new motorcycle. You can check out the manufacturers' Web sites, look for dealer Web sites, read road test reviews, participate in forum discussions about motorcycles you're interested in, chat in chat rooms, check dealer invoice prices, etc. You may even find dealers who will sell a motorcycle to you on the Web.

However, my personal opinion is that you should buy a new motorcycle from a dealer in a face-to-face situation. Even though you can save a few bucks by buying a bike 200 miles away, there is nothing like having a dealer close to your house with which you can establish a working relationship.

Buy from a dealer

Here are some tips on buying a new motorcycle from a dealer. If you are buying certain models that are in high demand, you may find dealers unwilling to budge on price. Some may even charge a premium over the MSRP for the bike.

Harley-Davidson dealers also have a product in great demand. They tend to fall into two camps: 1) Sell way over MSRP with short or no waiting period or 2) Sell close to MSRP with a long waiting period

The following buying tips may not work too well with motorcycles in high demand. If you want such a bike, you may have to shop around more and expect to pay a higher price than you would with other bikes.

Know what you want: Your motorcycle should fit your needs and you should look around and compare as much as possible before going in to see the dealer.

Do your homework: Understand what you want and talk to the salesperson about several different bikes that meet your needs. If you have narrowed your choice down to a couple of bikes, do the homework on all of the bikes. What do I mean by homework? Well, find out the dealer invoice price (this tells you how much the dealer pays for the motorcycle). Use an online service such as CycleCost.com to obtain a report on each bike. This report also tells how much the list price is (you can also go to the official Web site for the motorcycle manufacturer to get the list price). By getting the amount that the dealer pays for the motorcycle, you know his "ready to sell price." This tells you his automatic profit margin percentage. This should come out to be 10% - 15%. The dealer will do his best to make 10% total profit on the motorcycle.

Dealership Fees: All dealerships will include certain fees with the sale of the motorcycle. Most common fees are destination charges, setup fees, documentation fees, taxes, and maybe an assembly fee. The dealership also makes a profit on all these fees. There is no immediate way to find out their profit margin on these items but it should be between 5% - 15%.

Extras: The salesperson will also try to sell you motorcycle extras, for example, an extended warranty and accessories. The dealership makes a little on these too. These are specifically choice-driven. If you want it, you buy it.

Trade-Ins: As for trade-ins, do your homework here too. You can go to www.kbb.com (Kelly Blue Book) and find out the price of the vehicle either selling it outright or trading it in. The dealer will probably offer something under the blue book value of the motorcycle. You should also haggle about this too. Decide what's best for you. Do you want to make a few hundred dollars more and have to deal with the hassle of selling it yourself or do you just want to trade it in and not deal with all of the hassles.

The Negotiation: If you have decided on your bike and you have done your homework beforehand, you'll be ready to negotiate. In my opinion, a dealership has a goal of making about 10% profit on each deal. This means you may be able to talk them down substantially. It also helps if you buy an earlier model left-over new motorcycle. They want to free up the floor space and will be ready to deal. The longer it sits, the more it costs them and you will be helping to get older inventory out the door.

Paying for the Motorcycle: Most dealers are cash driven. Money in hand is the best form of tender there is. If you cannot pay cash, at least try to put down a big chunk of change. If financing, the larger the down payment, the less the monthly payments and the less interest you will pay. If you can, get a pre-approved loan from a lending institution so financing will not be a consideration. Often dealers will have special low-percentage loans available for certain models. These deals may influence your decision.

Getting the Most for your Current Bike: Your best move is to sell it privately rather than using it as a trade-in. Try to sell it before you buy the new motorcycle. In addition to the obvious financial benefit you'll derive from having only one motorcycle at a time to insure, maintain, etc., you won't feel pressure to come down on the price in order to sell your current ride quickly so you can meet a payment on the new bike.

Closing the Deal

Play Hardball with the Salesperson: The dealer wants to work with you. If they work with you, give them your other business such as apparel, repairs, and accessories. Try to emphasize that this is the start of a relationship, and they will try to work with you more.

Do your Homework: You are up against a pro in negotiations when you buy a motorcycle and lack of preparation will cost you big. After the deal is nearly done, you can almost always get them to sweeten it a little. A motorcycle helmet, cover or jacket can almost always be thrown in because after the salesperson has spent a good amount of time, they don't want to lose the sale.

The Bottom Line

There are many ways to buy a motorcycle. Use what works for you. The tips given here were compiled from various motorcycle forum postings by real motorcyclists giving their experiences in buying a motorcycle.

Good luck as you buy your next motorcycle.

Chapter 11

Buying a Motorcycle is Only the Beginning

Get ready to lay out a lot of cash to support your motorcycle habit

In the beginning there was the idea. Pretty innocuous at first: "I want to learn to ride a motorcycle." Just a simple goal, perhaps one that you've been thinking about a long time and finally have the family situation and money to accomplish. You encounter all the typical resistance from your family and friends but decide to go ahead anyway. You do it right. You buy a starter motorcycle and sign-up for a Motorcycle Safety Foundation (MSF) class. You find out after finishing the course that you really like to ride motorcycles so you continue your training with a good friend who has a lot of years of experience and has taken several MSF courses. Somewhere along the line you wake up one morning and realize that you have been bitten by the motorcycle bug and there is no cure.

Over the course of a year, you outgrow your first motorcycle and buy a bigger one.

Then after about six more months you decide you want to do some serious touring and want to cross several states. You end up needing to part with some serious cash to buy a new motorcycle. Now, when you just had the idea you wanted to ride back two years ago, you didn't realize that this need to ride would impact such a large part of your personal balance sheet. You find that a new touring bike is going to set you back as much as $18,000. Logic seems to have flown out the window by now so you find all kinds of ways to rationalize this purchase.

Also, you have had to upgrade your wardrobe by purchasing a helmet, boots, summer gloves, winter gloves, balaclava, wind triangle, denim jacket, leather motorcycle jacket with liner and vents, long winter riding suit, long underwear, electric vest, gloves, and socks, leather chaps, and numerous turtleneck pullovers. And, your buddy has a full leather riding suit that you've been eyeing and that's probably next.

As soon as you get the new motorcycle, you notice that they left something off. That piece of plastic on the side where the air from the engine comes out looks terrible. You run down to your dealer to buy a chrome replacement. On the way out the door, you see another customer's bike just like yours except it has a rack on the back trunk and what are those lights that go all the way around the bike? You don't have those. You run back in and inquire how you can get these features too. No problem. All it takes is cash. Are you beginning to get the picture? Your bike is fast becoming a money pit.

But this is only the beginning. As you travel around on your bike you see that other motorcyclists have customized their bikes in many beautiful and expensive ways. You find yourself drawn like a magnet to vendors who promise to add better performance to your bike's engine and suspension by buying their products. You find your backside is not dealing well with the stock seat and you have to decide among six different brands of custom seats. You're outgrowing your carrying capacity so you start investigating adding a trailer. The money is really flowing now.

Then one day your significant other comes up to you and says: "Honey, I want to get my own bike."

Well, double trouble is not what you expected when you set out on this journey to follow your dream. But, the die has been cast. Your life is over as you used to know it. All your children's inheritance is slipping fast.

The funny thing is you know your life has changed for the better. You've been places you never would have gone. You've met people you never would've met and had the best time of your life on your motorcycle.

In a way, you've been blessed in that now both of you are hooked into a new life of motorcycling. Yes, buying a bike is only the beginning and you will never be the same again.

Chapter 12

Motorcycle Trips and Touring

Learning how to take a trip or a long tour is usually evolutionary. First you learn to ride and then progressively start riding longer and longer distances. You carry just enough on the bike to survive. As the distances increase, you find you have to stay overnight. Thus, you begin to carry more and more on the bike and require more storage places. A tank bag is added, then saddlebags and then larger hard bags. You find that the bike is getting too small to carry what you need and still allow you to be comfortable on the machine. You purchase a larger bike, perhaps with a fairing and a trunk. You may be getting in the heavyweight class now such as a Honda Gold Wing, a Harley-Davidson dresser, a BMW touring bike, or other heavyweight tourer.

Touring is usually done in small groups but solo riding is popular too. Some even participate in guided tours and leave all the planning to experts. Many riders tour annually to special rallies such as the Sturgis Rally held in Sturgis, SD in August.

Before you go on a motorcycle trip, you need to determine if you have the right motorcycle, the right apparel, and the right physical conditioning to have a successful motorcycle trip. In addition, the bike must be in good mechanical condition. Further, you must determine what needs to be packed on the bike to make an enjoyable adventure. The kitchen sink is not required but often it seems to be the only thing left off. We discuss all aspects of getting ready to have a great motorcycle trip.

What's Your Motivation for Going?

A motorcycle trip is more than just a ride to the store for milk. A motorcycle trip is much longer. It might be 50 miles or 3000 miles or longer. It's a chance to go touring and see what's over the next hill.

You might be motivated by a chance remark by a friend to join them on a trip out West. You might read about a rally 300 miles away and want to go do some demo rides.

You could be motivated to ride somewhere beyond your limits. Your experience may be lacking or your bike's too small. You shouldn't go. Only the strong survive.

You might be wanting to test yourself. That's not all bad, if you're prepared.

Prepare the Motorcycle

Touring can be done on any motorcycle but these days, most touring riders want a big bike. When I thought about riding out West with friends, I was riding a Nighthawk 750 and my wife was on a Shadow 600. We quickly decided we needed new bikes to tour on. We bought twin Honda PC-800s. You have to decide what bike is best for your trip.

Once you know what bike, you need to make it mechanically perfect. Either do-it-yourself or let your local mechanic go over it. Change the fluids, buy new tires and battery, and get a good set of tools.

Of course, some riders are adventurers. They just ride and pray a lot.

Prepare Yourself

To take a long trip you should wear good quality protective apparel and a helmet. A trip can be dangerous. You don't know what will happen. Be prepared.

Riding 500 mile days takes a toll on the body. Join a health club and work out. I worked out for six months before I went on my 6000 mile trip.

Plan your route. Get a GPS if possible. Pick a few places to stay and make reservations. That will give you a goal to get there and keep you on schedule.

If you're going with friends, agree that you may disagree on the trip. Also, expect that your plans will change en route.

Plan to stay in touch with home. People worry.

Packing for the Trip

Some people are minimalists. They take a credit card, a change of clothing, and a bedroll. Others need to pull a trailer to haul their stuff. Most of us fall somewhere in between.

No matter what your requirements are, you need a packing list to keep track of what you need to bring and where it will be stored on the bike. Not to fear, I've devised a motorcycle packing list. I've used it on every trip I've ever gone. See the packing list in the Appendix.

You must also learn how to efficiently roll apparel into small shapes. Put items in sealed plastic bags if you expect rain. It always rains. Believe me, take a rain suit.

Consider Safety

We read about motorcycle accidents every day, some fatal. I spend a lot of time trying to tell riders to be safe while they ride. The fact is that most don't listen and think they are invincible, especially young riders. Do me a favor. Reread Chapter 10, "10 Ways to Be Safe on a Motorcycle," just before your trip. Some of my readers have told me that they hang up a copy of these 10 safety tips in their garages right over their bikes.

Remember that you are invisible out there and ride accordingly. Wear a helmet and protective gear. Slow down at intersections and watch out for oncoming drivers trying to turn left in front of you.

Consider What You Will Encounter on the Road

If you're used to riding to work over a well-known route, don't think that taking a long ride to a strange place over strange roads is going to be the same.

Our road system is a mine field of obstacles for motorcycles. You may encounter gravel in a blind turn, a hay wagon just as you crest a hill at 70 mph, or find yourself dodging mattresses that have just flown off a pickup truck ahead of you. Be alert and maintain space all around you to give you time to react.

Are you riding into the Plains states? Ever encountered a crosswind that leaned your bike over for 100 miles? You will.

Be prepared for anything.

Expect an Adventure

Taking a long trip on a motorcycle can be exhilarating. It will always be an adventure. It'll have its ups and downs but the worst day on a bike is better than the best day in a car, always.

When I toured 3000 miles in 2006, I wrote three blogs of my experiences. Some were embarrassing. Some involved injuries. I rode through lots of rain and got lost even with a GPS. I suffered from arthritis but made it through. My wife was in pain with a badly damaged knee (just successfully replaced). We rode with three separate groups of friends to three rallies. We had a blast.

Expect an adventure on your trip. You'll get it!

Chapter 13

Motorcycle Trikes

Riding on three wheels can be fun too

I got started late in motorcycling having ridden my first bike at age 51. I had a lot of catching up to do. My first bike was a 1981 Honda CM400T. Then came a 1991 Honda Nighthawk followed by a 1990 Honda Pacific Coast. I had looked longingly on Gold Wings since I first set foot in a Honda showroom but thought them ever too big for me to handle. In 1998 I decided that I finally was going to buy a new white Honda Gold Wing SE. I rode it for more than a year when my wife began having leg problems that made it difficult for her to hold up her PC-800. Something would have to be done to get her another bike that she could ride with her medical condition.

At an Americade Rally, I test rode a Motor Trike. This is a brand of motorcycle trike conversion that fits a variety of motorcycles. Motorcycle trikes are new to the general public and even some motorcyclists. Basically, a trike is a motorcycle with the rear wheel removed and replaced by two automotive wheels attached to a rear differential with shaft drive and wrapped in a fiberglass body. The result is a beautiful eye-catching machine that attracts people wherever it goes.

Trikes are not new. Harley-Davidson sold its Servi-Car 45ci trike between 1932 and 1972. Many were used by the police. You may also have seen them used as ice-cream wagons. Harley has recently realized that some of its most loyal customers were selling their Harleys and buying trikes from the competition. So, they came out with the Tri-Glide trike. You can actually buy a Harley-Davidson trike directly from a Harley dealer.

Also, many companies have been formed to sell trike conversion kits to fit most popular touring bikes.

Trikes have been made from car foundations as well, notably ones with VW engines.

A trike may have one wheel in front and two behind or two wheels in front and one behind. Most are steered with handlebars but some use steering wheels.

At Americade, Jeff Vey, CEO of Motor Trike, Inc., personally took people out for demo rides. Jeff is a stickler for technique. He lets you drive under his direction in a parking lot until he's convinced you can handle the trike. He let me take a Motor Trike out on the road. I rode it four miles up and back on a winding road. From this ride and the personal attention I received from Jeff, I decided to have my 1998 Gold Wing converted to a trike for my wife.

Jeff has his plant in Troup, TX but has a nationwide network of dealers who will do the conversion for you. I decided on Leola Motor Trike in PA.

When I went to pick up the completed trike, Ron Myers, the owner, told me war stories about mishaps that had occurred as people tried to drive their trikes home. Some ended up in the ditch across the street. One guy came back and pleaded with Ron to drive it back home for him. Hearing these stories, I was a little concerned about the trip back to New Jersey so I decided I would take back roads until I got more familiar with the trike.

I headed up Route 202 from the Lancaster, PA area. I hit almost every traffic light. I soon learned to love the fact that I didn't have to put my foot down at the stops. I didn't have to worry about balancing the bike as I stopped and started. I was beginning to enjoy myself. The metal-grate bridge over the Delaware River at New Hope, PA was a piece of cake. I even encountered lumber in the road in front of me and could easily steer over it without incident.

The hardest thing to do was unlearn some of the skills I used for riding on 2-wheels. On a motorcycle, you push the left handlebar forward to go left and the right handlebar forward to go right. That's called countersteering. On a trike, it's just the opposite. If you're traveling 60 mph in the fast lane on a bike and you see an obstruction ahead, you instinctively push the right handlebar forward to veer the bike to the right. If you encounter the same situation on a trike and you let your instincts take over, you will turn the trike directly across the center line into oncoming traffic. That's precisely what happened to me after about two hours into the trip. I was whipping along about 50 mph and was suddenly aware that I was headed straight for an oncoming truck after I had a mental lapse. It was a bit unnerving.

I also found I had to slow down to get through sharp curves. Once I was in a curve, I had to continue to push with force to keep the bike in the lane. I knew there must be a technique for taking these curves but I hadn't figured it out at that time.

Well, my overall impression of the Motor Trike was positive. I was able to drive it 135 miles without hitting anything and I only had one close-call.

Recently I met two trikers who had never ridden a motorcycle at all. They took to triking right off since they didn't have any residual skills to unlearn or modify.

My guess is that more people will be taking up trikes. Some of these people will be old-time motorcyclists who gave up riding years ago because of injuries. Some will be people like me who are tired of balancing a bike in heavy stop-and-go traffic and want to enjoy motorcycling without being worn out at the end of the day.

Riding on three wheels can take some learning

As I mentioned, the real reason I wanted to have the Gold Wing converted was to provide a trike for my wife. She had a few medical problems that caused her quite a bit of pain when using her leg for riding. I felt that converting the Wing would provide her with a stable platform where she could continue riding.

I'm finding more and more motorcyclists opting for a trike so they can continue enjoying the sport even though they may have some disabilities.

My wife did have a few problems learning to ride the trike. She had never ridden a Gold Wing and was not used to the feel of the clutch and throttle. She drove the trike down the drive, tried to turn right but was too wide and so she chose to turn left. She went to the first cross street and did a U-turn narrowly missing the curb and proceeded up the street to a park entrance just two houses up from us.

She turned the bike right into the driveway but didn't have the wheels straightened when she gave the trike too much throttle. The bike veered to the left, climbed the curb onto the grass and knocked down a pole and sign before she could get the presence of mind to stop it. Needless to say, she was a bit discouraged and embarrassed by her maiden voyage.

There was damage to the bike but it was still rideable. She was able to get in about 30 minutes of practice in the parking lot that same day which restored her confidence a little.

After that, she practiced on the trike with me on the PC-800 while we communicated by CB. She didn't make any more mistakes. We started riding in the neighborhood, then on the local highway, then through heavy traffic, and finally on a high-speed road at 65 mph. I was confident that she would be able to handle the trike. It would just take more practice.

Since then, my wife did very well with the trike and even rode it to Massachusetts to take a special trike rider education class sponsored by the Gold Wing Road Riders Association (GWRRA).

A picture of the completed Motor Trike is shown above.

Becoming a 2-trike family

I took many trips with my wife on her white trike. Sometimes I was on the PC-800 and other times I was on my new red 2000 Honda Gold Wing SE. She loved to make quick turns into shopping centers or whip around a hairpin turn and decide to pull off the road to take a picture. On these occasions I found myself usually fighting just to keep the bike upright and check out the traffic around me when all of a sudden she was off the road and I was trying to figure out how best to get off the road and find a decent parking place all the time balancing the 900+ pounds of the Wing.

Once, we were on a lighthouse tour in New Jersey. The last lighthouse we were to visit was the East Point Lighthouse near Cape May. This lighthouse was really off the beaten path. As we got within a mile of the place, suddenly there was a road crew ahead of us grading the road. One side was torn up and the other was being filled with dirt. This was the only road to the lighthouse.

There was no way I was going to chance taking my new Gold Wing down that road. However, I told my wife to go ahead and try it on the trike. Of course, there was no problem with the trike with those massive rear tires. I think it was at that point that I mentally threw in the towel and decided that I was going to get a trike for myself.

In early October, 2000, I contracted with Leola Motor Trike in PA to do the trike conversion. They had done the white trike for my wife. In early November, I was still waiting for the trike kit to be shipped from the Motor Trike plant in Texas. Then on November 6 I got the call from Leola that they would be coming that day to haul my Wing away to be converted. I got the trike delivered back to my house on December 7.

Road testing the red trike

After I got the trike, I took it out for a short 15 mile ride just to check for basic operation. I also took the trike to a parking lot and did a series of figure-eights just to get some practice on turning the machine. That was followed by some stops and starts and swerving maneuvers.

Turning a trike requires that you push the handlebars quite a lot forward. There is NO leaning involved or countersteering. To go right, you push the left handlebar grip forward. To go left, you push the right handlebar grip forward. These actions are just the opposite of what's required on a motorcycle. It obviously takes a little mind-training to orient yourself to a trike. When sitting on the trike, it "looks" like a motorcycle. Your mind tells you that you're sitting on a motorcycle. All the controls are the same as a motorcycle. The only problems are that the trike will not lean, it will not countersteer and you can't put your foot down when you stop. Some have been known to have their foot run over by doing so.

After that early ride, I took the trike out twice to ride to Polar Bear Grand Tour meetings. I put about 150 miles on the trike riding at speeds up to 65 mph.

The trike was equipped with gas shocks and a so-called airbag suspension system that's hooked up to the standard Gold Wing air compressor system.

The trike used BF Goodrich Radial T/A tires, 235R 60 X 15. It came with a three-year or 36,000 mile warranty.

I ordered mine with a trailer hitch, Roadhawk wheels with spinner upgrade, Ring-of-Fire lights on the front wheel, front fork lights, master cylinder light switch to control all new lights, wind deflectors, ISO highway boards, ISO pegs, tombstone tail lights with gold eagle red lens on top, license light bar, lower rear bumper with Kuryakyn lights and shields, lighted mud flaps, trunk rack, trike cover, trunk liner, and trunk rack bag. Oh, and I tossed in a change holder too.

The best things about the trike are that you no longer need to be concerned about metal-grated bridges, snow packed roads, parking lots and gas stations with ice and snow, continual stopping and starting in heavy traffic, gravel and stone parking lots and driveways, losing your balance if you have to make a quick stop and tipping your trike over while stopped.

The new things to worry about are learning that you are not on a bike anymore and remembering that the trike is wide and you have to compensate when you pull in next to a gasoline island or a toll plaza. You also get poorer gas mileage -- 30 instead of 38 mpg. There are also more mechanical concerns since you now have half motorcycle and half car. There are more problems being delayed while traveling since almost no one has ever seen a trike before and they all come running over to ask questions -- some even yell questions to you out of their car windows and some cars have been known to drift into your lane as they try to "look you over." Also, you have to remember to leave the trike in gear when you park it or risk having it roll away. Some trikers purchase a hand brake for this purpose.

While cruising at a steady 65 mph, the trike is highly stable. Cross-winds don't normally affect you but a passing truck will be noticed. Easy highway turns are simple to negotiate. A light touch on the handlebar grips with easy motions will take you anywhere. Tight turns or decreasing radius turns on entrance and exit ramps are noticeably more difficult and require steady pressure. Lines through curves are recommended but this is a technique best learned by practice. I'm told by the CEO of Motor Trike, that a good trike rider can beat a good motorcycle rider through Deal's Gap knowing the proper technique. I have more practice ahead of me on that one.

Most trikes are built on the Gold Wing 1500 platform since it is readily available, very stable, has sufficient power and a low center of gravity. There is also a new option of a fuel cell that will add an additional 3 1/2 gallons of fuel. The Classic II trunk on my trike is supposed to have the same capacity as the two saddlebags normally fitted to the Gold Wing.

As mentioned before, the biggest difficulty with becoming familiar with a trike is getting used to the steering. I'm not kidding when I say that most of the trike accidents occur right after the owner takes possession and drives off thinking he or she is on a motorcycle. It's a really weird sensation the first time you try to pull over to the right by pushing the right handlebar grip and find yourself headed straight for an 18-wheeler in the oncoming lane. You've been warned!

You must steer a trike like a car. There is no steering wheel so you have to imagine that the handlebars are just part of a huge steering wheel that's been cut off at the bottom. If I see I have to make a right hand turn ahead, I think of pushing the left handlebar grip forward toward the direction of the turn. If I see a left hand turn coming, I think of pushing the right handlebar grip forward toward the direction of the turn. I'm told this will become second nature with practice. I do know that I can easily get off the trike, hop on a 2-wheeler, and ride it with no problems. I guess the imprinted motorcycle program is ingrained.

I did learn an important riding technique from my wife. After many failed attempts to keep up with her on mountain curves, I finally realized that she was steering the trike differently from me. The easiest way to steer a trike is to pull the handlebar grip back. To turn right, pull the right handlebar grip back toward you. You can also help the turn by also pushing the left handlebar grip forward away from you but the main emphasis should be on pulling. And, of course, to turn left, pull the left handlebar grip back toward you. This technique will keep you out in front with the best riders.

Motorcycle trikes are strange and exciting 3-wheel motorcycles

A strange new motorcycle has recently been seen by some motorists: a motorcycle trike. They encounter it at gas pumps and on the interstate highways. They see the motorcycle trike glistening way up ahead on the road and can't quite figure out what it is. They speed up to get a better look.

Kids roll down the windows and yell, "Hey, what is that thing?"

The owner of this likeable 3-wheeled vehicle just smiles back and says, "It's a trike."

For most people this is not enough information. If they happen to see you standing next to your trike at a gas pump or in a parking lot, they come over briskly before you know they're there and barrage you with questions. If you desire the solitary life with your motorcycle, never convert it to a trike.

I knew that trikes were attention-getters but you really find out when you own one.

When I converted my white 1998 Honda Gold Wing SE motorcycle to a trike for my wife, I found that I was totally ignored and everyone was drawn to her trike as if it were a magnet. Then when I found that the advantages of a trike were starting to become more obvious to me, I decided to convert my own 2000 Honda Gold Wing SE to a trike also. Double trouble! Now we had to field questions about both conversions.

The following are the stock motorcycle trike questions we get asked all the time. Please memorize these so you can help inform your own friends and family should you come upon a trike minding its own business:

Q: "How much does that cost?"

A: "First you have to buy a Gold Wing motorcycle for $15-20K and then get a trike conversion done. That could cost you as much as $9K more."

Q: "Can I buy one of those?"

A: "Yes, if you can find one for sale already put together. Otherwise, you'll have to have a trike conversion done on a Gold Wing motorcycle. The cost? See question, above."

Q: "Who makes that?"

A: "There are a number of trike conversion companies with dealers scattered across the USA and Canada. Honda doesn't make it. They only provide the motorcycle part. You have to add the back part from a trike conversion company. They remove the rear wheel and saddlebags and bolt-on the rear section consisting of two wide automotive wheels, a differential and new driveshaft, fenders, and rear trunk. They paint it to match the colors of the bike."

Q: "Can you buy a trike kit for a Harley or something different from Honda?"

A: "Yes."

Q: "I heard that 3-wheelers were unstable and were banned."

A: "That was the old 3-wheel ATVs that Honda made that were tipping over. These new motorcycle trikes have a low center of gravity, a 6-cylinder engine, a shaft drive, extremely wide rear tires and are very stable under all conditions encountered on the road."

Trikes have many advantages over regular motorcycles including:

- You don't have to put your feet down when you stop.
- You can take a passenger without fear that you will tip over the bike and spill the passenger into the road. Most significant others like this feature. Some wives, in fact, have refused to ride pillion with their husbands until they converted their bike to a trike.

Trikes do have some disadvantages over motorcycles:

- They get poorer gas mileage.
- You have to make sure you get it in gear when stopped or it may roll away to parts unknown.
- You have to remember that the rear end is wider than the front or you may run into the island at your favorite gas station or toll booth.

Some riders want to have their cake and eat it too. They want to be able to ride their trike and then, just like superman, have it magically convert into a bike when they want to ride on 2-wheels. These folks are riding the Voyager conversion that looks like a trike but in a few minutes can be changed back to a bike. Very devious.

Here are a few more comments I've heard on the road about trikes:

"I used to have a Servi-Car."

"Now, I could ride that."

"That is so beautiful."

"Did you see that motorcycle? It had 3-wheels. Like a motorcycle with training wheels."

Are you ready for a trike?

This chapter has discussed motorcycle trikes based on my personal experience with two of them. You most likely will start your motorcycling career on a 2-wheel motorcycle. It will serve you well if you get proper training, wear proper riding apparel, and ride with safety in mind. Many riders say they would give up motorcycling if their only option was to ride a trike. I have seen many change their minds when a sudden disability beset them. Riding is too important to most of us who have been around motorcycles for a while. Not riding is not an option for me and I think you may agree at some point in your riding career. Triking is here to stay. You too may find a trike in your future.

Acknowledgments

I would like to thank all the motorcyclists I have ever met. They gave me answers when I needed them. They encouraged me with their enthusiasm for motorcycling. They picked my spirit up by waving back at me when I approached them on the road. They instilled in me a new sense of freedom as I rode. They helped me every time I asked and sometimes even when I didn't.

The cover design was crafted by Debbie Simpkins who works on a tight deadline quite well

I especially wish to thank Rosemarie who has ridden with me in recent years and provides me freedom to squirrel myself away to write for long periods of time.

About the Author

Walter Kern spent 35 years as an electrical engineer for Bell
Laboratories. After he retired in 1996, he built Websites for a
while, then signed on at About.com as its Motorcycles Guide.
There he started with a 3-page site and built it to one with more
than 20,000 pages. After leaving About in 2007, he founded the
Motorcycle Views Web site (motorcycleviews.com). He also
manages the Polar Bear Grand Tour Web site
(polarbeargrandtour.com) and takes all their weekly pictures. He
took up motorcycling at the age of 51 together with his wife, Jane,
who also rode her own motorcycle. He currently rides a 2000
Honda Gold Wing SE Motor Trike, is a pet parent to an eight
pound Maltipoo dog named Princee, and writes a lot at a new
home in Florida with his fiancée, Rosemarie.

Appendix 1 - Glossary

2-Second Rule: This is the minimum spacing in seconds between moving motorcycles. While in formation, maintain a 2-second interval from the rider in front of you. Measure the time by counting "one-thousand one, one-thousand two" as you see the rider in front of you pass a sign or landmark. Stop counting when you pass the same marker. Under poor weather conditions, maintain longer intervals consistent with safety.

2-Stroke: A 2-Stroke is an engine (also known as a Stroker) having two strokes per cycle. The combustion stroke occurs when the piston moves down allowing the exhaust gases to exit through an opening. The compression stroke is the upward movement of the piston where the air-fuel mixture is drawn in and the spark plug ignites the mixture causing an explosion, thereby forcing the piston back down again. (Also Known As: Stroker, 2-Cycle)

4-Stroke: A 4-Stroke is an engine that uses four strokes to complete a complete cycle. The four strokes are: Intake, Compression, Combustion, and Exhaust. During the **Intake Stroke**, the intake valve opens and an air-fuel mixture enters the chamber above the piston. The piston moves down drawing the mixture in. The intake valve then closes and the piston moves up for the **Compression Stroke** compressing the mixture. The spark plug then ignites the mixture causing an explosion. The resulting force moves the piston down again for the **Combustion Stroke**. Then the exhaust valve opens as the piston moves upward for the **Exhaust Stroke** and all the exhaust gases are ported through the exhaust system. Also Known As: 4-Cycle.

ABATE: ABATE is a biker organization that promotes more freedom for motorcyclists by limiting restrictive laws that affect riders. ABATE has organizations in most states. The name of the organization varies from state to state. It is known by "Alliance of Bikers Aimed Toward Education," "A Brotherhood Aimed Toward

Education," and "American Bikers Aimed Toward Education." There may be other variations. ABATE keeps track of what state legislatures are doing relative to motorcycling and rallies its members to support legislation in the best interests of bikers. ABATE has devoted much of its resources to helmet laws.

ABS: ABS stands for Anti-lock Braking System. The system, popularized on BMW and then Honda ST1100 motorcycles, utilizes a computerized system to sense wheel lockup and then release and reapply the brakes many times per second. The result is a steady controlled braking without skidding. Most experienced riders can stop a motorcycle faster by fully utilizing the front and rear brakes with steady controlled pressure just short of a lockup. Anyone attending a motorcycle rally has probably seen the famous BMW demonstration where they flood a parking lot and then ride a BMW without ABS, but containing outriggers, through the water and make a panic stop. The result is a tip over onto the outriggers. Next, a BMW with ABS is run through the same course and this time, the ABS causes the bike to make a controlled straight line stop.

Air Cleaner: An Air Cleaner is a filtering device with a replaceable cartridge (air filter) that filters the incoming air to the fuel system on the motorcycle engine.

Airhead: Airhead refers to the air-cooled engines of early BMW motorcycles.

AMA: American Motorcyclist Association - 260,000 motorcyclist members

Americade: Touring Rally held in the first full week of June at Lake George, NY

AMF: AMF stands for American Machine and Foundry which is a well-known company that once owned Harley-Davidson from 1969-1981.

Ape Hangers: If you remember the motorcycles in the movie Easy Rider, you may also remember that the riders held onto handlebars that were above their shoulders. The position of the rider is almost like an ape hanging from a tree, hence the term, Ape Hangers.

Arenacross: Arenacross is a variant of Supercross performed inside athletic arenas. These shows are promoted by large companies and attract large audiences and TV coverage. The jumps are more spectacular and closer to the audience.

Arlen Ness: Motorcycle customizing owes much to the talents of Arlen Ness. He started out in 1967 by customizing his own Harley-Davidson Knucklehead. It won first place in the first custom show he entered. Soon he was doing custom bikes for a long line of customers and continued to win awards living by the slogan, "Always innovate, never imitate." His latest creation is the Arlen Ness Signature Series for Victory motorcycles.

Automatics: Riders of motorcycles are used to shifting gears and using a clutch. However, some new riders would like to do away with shifting and clutching since they may have become used to automatic transmissions in cars. They often ask if they can buy an Automatic motorcycle. Well, in the early '80s, Honda made an Automatic. They called it the Hondamatic. These days, most scooters come with automatic transmissions as well as a few motorcycles such as the Boss Hoss and the Ridley. You still can't get an automatic on a Honda Gold Wing even though it seems to have just about everything else.

Bagger: A Bagger is a motorcycle that is fitted with Saddlebags to allow the rider to carry items for a trip. Many start riding with no particular way to carry anything of any size. Some will resort to strapping on luggage to a Sissy Bar or by means of a Bungee Cord. Others go for saddlebags. The term may also apply to any Touring Bike.

Balaclava: A Balaclava is a thin pull-over head and neck cover with eye slits for winter usage under a motorcycle helmet. Pronunciation: Bal-A-Clav'-A (noun)

Basketcase: A Basketcase is a pile of parts usually bought as a whole and supposedly from a single bike model. Basketcases are bought especially by motorcycle restorers to help finish out a restoration.

Battery: A Battery is an electrical storage device that forms the central core of a motorcycle's electrical system. Most modern batteries are 12 volts. Many riders use trickle chargers to maintain their battery. Batteries may require periodic servicing but many are maintenance-free. When a battery fails on the road, the rider may want to jump-start the battery. It's probably a good idea to replace a battery every two years.

Beanie: A beanie, also called a shortie, is a small motorcycle helmet that sits on the top of the head providing less protection than other helmets. Some beanies are not made to safety standards and used mainly for show.

Beater: Beginning riders should not attempt to buy a new motorcycle as their first bike. Almost always, a new rider will take a spill or two on their first motorcycle and cause some physical damage. It's better if they have an old bike that they can learn on and won't cost much to fix. Such a bike is often referred to as a Beater. The term may come from the same source that produced the beat-up car.

Beemer: A term used for a BMW motorcycle. A Bimmer is the corresponding term used for a BMW automobile.

Belt Drive: Belt Drive is a method to transmit power from the transmission to the rear wheel of the motorcycle using a belt. The belt requires practically no maintenance. Harley-Davidson has used Belt-Drive systems on most of its motorcycles in recent years.

Bike Blessing: Since motorcycling is an activity involving risk, it is sometimes prudent to bless these machines and their riders before a group ride. These are called Bike Blessings or a Blessing of the Bikes. Bike Blessings are informal religious ceremonies conducted by ministers, priests, rabbis, and other religious authorities. Some Bike Blessings involve thousands of bikes. Others may involve only a few bikes. Bike Blessings were performed one-bike-at-a-time, upon request, at the BuRP Rally held in Maggie Valley, NC. The BuRP rally is organized and run by members of various motorcycle forums including the Motorcycle Views Forum.

Biker: A Biker is one who rides a bike or motorcycle. The term Biker brings up different images to different people. Biker has an edge to it that speaks to a lifestyle. The term Motorcyclist is used interchangeably at times but Motorcyclist doesn't seem to have the same edge. A lifestyle change may not be as pronounced as with the term Biker.

Blue Knights: The Blue Knights® is a non-profit fraternal organization consisting of active and retired law enforcement men and women who enjoy riding motorcycles.

BMW: BMW is a brand of motorcycle. BMWs were first made in 1923 with the R32 boxer. If you mention BMW to most non-riders, you will almost always hear, "I didn't know BMW made motorcycles." Actually, they made motorcycles before they made cars.

Bottom End: Bottom End refers to the bottom portion of a motorcycle engine including the crankshaft, connecting rods and bearings, primary chain, cam sprockets, seals, and other components that support delivering the power to the transmission and rear wheel of the machine.

Boxer: Refers to the BMW R-Series engine that has two horizontally opposed cylinders.

Bungee Cord: Bungee cords or nets are used to secure cargo to a bike. There are U-shaped hooks at the ends of the cords that fasten around various parts of the bike as anchors.

BuRP Rally: The BuRP Rally is a motorcycle rally founded by members of various motorcycle forums. BuRP stands for Blue Ridge Parkway and You. The rally was first held in 2002, basically as a ride by forum members. In subsequent years, the rally has been based in Maggie Valley, NC and includes rides on the Blue Ridge Parkway, Deal's Gap, and other scenic roads. The organizers of the BuRP rally are on the Motorcycle Views Forum.

Cafe Racer: A Cafe Racer is a style of bike popularized in London in the '50s where bikers wanted a fast, personalized and distinctive bike to travel from cafe to cafe. Many Cafe Racer bikes have distinctive small low-cut Fairings.

Cage: An automobile. On a motorcycle you are exposed to the environment and nature. You're free. In a car you are isolated, enclosed, and separated from the environment and nature. It's as if you are locked in a cage.

Caliper: A Caliper is the non-rotating portion of the motorcycle Disc Brake that contains the hydraulic components including the brake pads. The Caliper is positioned on both sides of the Rotor such that as the brakes are applied, the brake pads are pressed against both sides of the Rotor, thereby stopping the motorcycle.

Camshaft: A Camshaft is a shaft containing lobes (also called cams) which is synchronized with the crankshaft. Its function is to rotate and open and close the valves in the engine. Camshafts may be located on top of the heads of the engine (SOHC or DOHC) or near the crankshaft. When the camshaft is located near the crankshaft, its rotation causes its lobes to press on Pushrods which extend to the top of the engine and connect to rocker arms which then open and close the valves. Harley-Davidson motorcycles are heavy users of the pushrod method of valve operation.

CB: The Citizen's Band (CB) radio craze in automobiles has long since died but CBs are still used to communicate especially by motorcyclists. Most heavyweight touring motorcycles are equipped with CBs today. CBs have 40 channels and a range of several miles under good conditions. They are used in tour groups at major rallies to maintain motorcycle-to-motorcycle communications.

CC: CC refers to the cubic centimeters of Displacement of an engine. Usually written, for example, as 1200cc. Total engine displacement is the volume displaced by a piston in a cylinder during a single stroke, multiplied by the number of cylinders.

Centerstand: A Centerstand is a stand mounted under the motorcycle with a spring return. When the Centerstand is extended to the ground, it holds the motorcycle vertical with the rear wheel just off the ground. Such a stand is useful for leveling the bike and spinning the rear wheel to lube the chain (if used). It also makes a nice platform if you want to park your bike at the curb at a rally and watch all the other bikes go by. Not all motorcycles have centerstands but do have Sidestands.

Chain Drive: A Chain Drive is a method to transmit power from the transmission to the rear wheel of the motorcycle using a chain. The chain is much like that on a bicycle requiring periodic lubrication -- a messy job.

Chaps: Most motorcycle riders like to have some protection on their legs while riding. A pair of leather chaps does the trick. Chaps usually have snaps near the ankles and a zipper down the legs. They're pulled around the waist like a belt and fastened. The backside is open.

Choke: The Choke is a device that restricts the air intake to result in a richer fuel mixture which assists in starting the engine. Most motorcycles have knobs or levers to pull out to decrease the air intake. After the engine has warmed up, the choke may be pushed back in. Warm motorcycle engines normally do not require choking to restart.

Chopper: A Cruiser style bike that has a lot of the pieces of the bike "chopped off." The riders of the '60s did everything they could to customize their bikes and make them go faster. Thus, much of the existing bikes they bought were chopped off. The bikes in the movie *Easy Rider* are examples of choppers.

CI: CI refers to the Cubic Inches of Displacement of an engine. Usually written, for example, as 80ci. Total engine displacement is the volume displaced by a piston in a cylinder during a single stroke, multiplied by the number of cylinders.

Clip-ons: Clip-Ons are special handlebars that clamp on. They provide a lower, more forward riding position. The forward shifting of the weight of the rider often results in better handling of the bike.

Clutch - Dry: A Dry Clutch is more like the clutch found on an automobile that separates the engine from the transmission. There is a dry connection between the engine and transmission. See also Wet Clutch term.

Clutch - Wet: A Wet Clutch is one that contains many plates that are in the oil spray of the transmission and the oil gets between the plates. The plates on wet clutches have a tendency to stick together when the bike sits. So, when you start the bike in the morning, before you put it in first gear to move off, depress the clutch lever for about 30 seconds to allow the oil on the plates to drain off and the plates to separate. Otherwise, you'll get a decided clunk and slight movement forward when you put it in first. See also Dry Clutch term.

Colors: Many bikers / motorcyclists join motorcycle clubs. Usually these clubs have distinctive jackets. Also, clubs will issue club patches to display on the jackets. These patches and sometimes the jacket design itself are known as Colors. In certain motorcycle clubs there may be disputes over territory and the wording and arrangement of the various elements of the Colors. You may hear that certain establishments don't want any Colors displayed by bikers so that such disputes will not occur. The subject of Colors is a complex one and subject to considerable debate on motorcycle forums.

Compression Ratio: Here's a definition from Motorcycle Views forum moderator, Bill Wood:

> "Think of Compression Ratio this way: When the piston is at the bottom of the cylinder, say you could pour 100cc of water into the spark plug hole (both valves closed) and it would be full. When the piston is at the top of its stroke, you can only pour 10cc of water into the hole to fill it. The compression ratio would be 100 to 10 or 10 to 1. That's about as easy to understand as I can make it. Oops, forgot to say -- Higher compression ratios (in general) will let the engine make more power, require higher octane gas and be harder for the starter to turn over."

Contact Patch: The Contact Patch (CP) is the area on the ground where your motorcycle tire actually touches the road surface. This area can be very small and highlights the fact that there isn't much actual contact between your bike and the road.

Co-Rider: Motorcyclist riding on the back of a motorcycle behind the rider. The co-rider is an active participant and assists the rider during certain maneuvers. Could also be someone riding in a sidecar. See also Pillion term.

Countersteer: A motorcycle turns left/right by slightly pushing the left/right handlebar. Push left, go left. Push right, go right. This is called countersteering.

Crash Bar: Many motorcycles have a Crash Bar or guard to protect the bike should it fall over. You'll have to look carefully on some bikes to see them and not all bikes are so equipped. Some models hide the protectors behind plastic covers. Look for extended areas on the bike where the guards may be hiding. For Newbies, a Crash Bar may be the only thing standing in the way of an expensive repair job that could cost you hundreds of dollars because of a simple tip over.

Crotch Rocket: A term some people use to describe a high-performance Sportbike motorcycle. If you want to know more about the real world of sportbikes and forget about the commonly used term, Crotch Rocket, check out a good sportbike forum. These forums allow you to converse with real sportbike riders and racers. We also don't encourage new riders to buy sportbikes as their first bike. It's better to buy a cheap bike to learn on. A new sportbike is fast, touchy, and doesn't have much margin for error. It also costs a lot to repair when you tip it over while you're learning to ride.

Cruiser: The modern version of the Chopper with small gas tank, large rear tire, and feet forward seating and stylish appearance accounts for about 33 percent of all sales.

Custom Motorcycles: For many motorcyclists, the choices provided by the motorcycle manufacturers do not provide enough variety to match the personalities of the riders. For this reason, many customize their motorcycles or hire customizers to do the work for them. Many of these custom motorcycles are entered in shows and win prizes. Motorcycle Customs can easily cost twice the selling price of the original bike.

Daytona: The famous Daytona Bike Week held in late February to early March in Daytona Beach, FL.

Desmodromic: Desmodromic has to do with valve control in the engine. With desmodromic control, no return springs are used and the engine relies on compression to seat the valves. This is a design used previously by Mercedes and others but became an integral part of the Ducati motorcycle engine. It allowed for much higher rpm and Horsepower and immediately proved itself in racing. See the book, *Ducati*, for illustrations of the Desmo valve control system and a description of its operating principles.

Dirt Bike: Some motorcycles are designed to be ridden on rough terrain. They are known as Dirt Bikes or trail bikes. Dirt bikes will typically have suspension with more travel than a street bike, higher ground clearance, and a small (less than 500cc) engine. Related to dirt bikes are Dual-sport bikes which are street-legal versions of dirt bikes with more suspension travel than a standard bike but having all the other equipment usually found on street bikes.

Disc Brake: A Disc Brake consists of both a rotating portion called the Rotor and a stationary portion called the Caliper. The Rotor is attached to the wheel of the motorcycle. The Caliper assembly parts work against the Rotor to apply pressure to it thereby stopping the wheel from turning. It's difficult to say precisely when the components of a disc brake should be replaced since so much depends on how the motorcyclist uses the brakes.

Displacement: Displacement is the volume displaced in the cylinders of an engine as the pistons move from their bottom position to their highest position in the cylinders. Displacement is measured in either cubic centimeters (cc) or cubic inches (ci).

DOHC: DOHC stands for Double OverHead Camshaft. In a DOHC engine, each head of the engine has two overhead Camshafts to operate the valves for that head. This is done so that multiple valves per cylinder can be opened and closed by the camshaft.

DOT Helmet Rating: The Department of Transportation (DOT) rates motorcycle helmets. The rating is based on dropping the helmet containing a simulated head from a height of 10 feet. The "head" must receive no more than 400 Gs over a prescribed dwell time. See Bill Stermer's book, *Motorcycle Touring and Travel*, for more information.

Drag Bars: Drag Bars are distinctive custom handlebars that are relatively straight and require a slight forward leaning to reach. The look is great but some complain about difficult low-speed handling. You may need long arms to have a successful experience using Drag Bars.

Dresser: Normally a large fully equipped motorcycle with Fairing, Saddlebags, and a trunk.

Drum Brake: A Drum Brake is the older style of motorcycle brake. Most bikes use Disc Brakes these days. Drum brakes work by forcing brake shoes against the inside of a rotating drum that is part of the wheel. Many motorcycle trikes use drum brakes for rear brakes.

Dual-Sport: Dual-Sport refers to a street-legal motorcycle that is designed to also be used in Off-Road situations. Thus if one were planning a trip to South America, it might be wise to ride a dual-sport bike to be ready for any road conditions.

Easy Rider: The famous motorcycle movie, released in 1969, starring Peter Fonda, Dennis Hopper, and Jack Nicholson

EFI: Electronic Fuel Injection (EFI) is a fuel delivery mechanism that eliminates the need for a carburetor. A computerized control system accounts for elevation changes and delivers the necessary information to the EFI system to change the air-to-fuel mixture to achieve optimal fuel economy and engine performance.

Electrics: Many motorcyclists ride in all kinds of weather conditions. Thus, riding is not just for fair weather. Some motorcyclists ride when it gets cold and sometimes regular apparel just isn't enough to keep warm. That's when riders use electric apparel referred to as Electrics. Most start with electric vests, then electric gloves and then electric pants or suits. Some even go for electric socks. These electric apparel contain heating elements and are usually controlled by thermostats connected to the motorcycle's Battery.

Enduro: According to the rules of the AMA, "An Enduro is a meet in which speed is not the determining factor and a time schedule must be maintained. It takes place on a variety of terrain, little-used roads and trails, etc." Enduros can be as long as 60-100 miles and require considerable skill and endurance to complete.

Engine Guards: Many motorcycles have Engine Guards to protect the bike should it fall over. These are billed as Engine Guards but sometimes they are referred to as Crash Bars. We don't want to emphasize crashing a motorcycle since that is not a desired result and proper training should minimize the possibility of any crash.

You'll have to look carefully on some bikes to see the engine guards and not all bikes are so equipped. Some models hide the protectors behind plastic covers. Look for extended areas on the bike where the guards may be hiding. For Newbies, an Engine Guard may be the only thing standing in the way of an expensive repair job that could cost you hundreds of dollars because of a simple tip over.

Enrichener: The Enrichener injects an extra amount of fuel to assist in starting the motorcycle. If the Throttle is opened, the function of the enrichener is defeated. The effect of the enrichener is to provide extra fuel to assist starting. This is similar to the function of the Choke but the choke only restricts air intake (which has the effect of making the mixture richer in fuel). The enrichener has been used by BMW and Harley-Davidson. Most motorcycles have knobs or levers to pull out to decrease the air intake for chokes or increase the fuel intake for enricheners. After the engine has warmed up, the enrichener may be pushed back in.

Evolution: Evolution is the name of the Harley-Davidson engine used from 1984-1999, sometimes called the EVO. The engine is a 45 degree V-Twin displacing 80ci/1340cc. Check out the Harley-Davidson Web site to see pictures of their engines.

E-ZPass: Motorcyclists have always had a problem at toll plazas. They have to slow down, push up their face shields, stop, shift into neutral (sometimes even put the sidestand down and kill the engine because neutral couldn't be found), remove their gloves, search for their toll ticket and change, hand to the toll taker, receive change, put their gloves back on, (possibly retract the sidestand and restart the bike), shift to first, and move off.

Well, many highway authorities are using electronic toll collection methods to speed traffic through toll plazas and that has become pure pleasure for riders of motorcycles. The names of these computerized systems vary depending on where you are. In the East, the system used is called E-ZPass. This system covers most of the major toll roads in NJ, DE, PA, NY, MA, WV, and MD.

Just sign-up and receive a small flat tag for your windshield. Pass through the E-ZPass toll plaza at low speed and the system reads your E-ZPass tag and subtracts money out of your account to pay the toll.

Some E-ZPass toll plazas are designed to allow high-speed traffic so you can ride your bike at near speed-limit rates through the lane. These lanes are identified as express lanes at the outside edges of the toll plaza complex with no barriers on the sides of the lane.

If you have such a system near you and you use the toll roads a lot, get signed up and then you can concentrate on riding and not stopping.

Fairing: An enclosure on the front of the motorcycle containing the windshield and affording wind protection to the rider. Can be attached to the frame and not move or be attached to the fork and move as the handlebars are turned.

Fat Boy®: Harley-Davidson released a motorcycle in 1990 based on the FLST Heritage Softail. They called it the FLSTF or Fat Boy. It is immediately recognized by its solid cast disc front wheel.

FIM: FIM, the Fédération Internationale de Motocyclisme, is the world-wide motorcycle sanctioning body based in Geneva, Switzerland. The AMA is the sole U.S affiliate to the FIM. The FIM is comprised of nearly 70 national organizations (called Federations) from countries around the world. The FIM establishes and enforces racing rules and calendars for all types of international competition, ranging from Motocross and road racing to Trials and Enduros.

Flathead: Flathead is a type of engine where the valves are located in the side of the engine. The head of the engine is flat with just a place for the spark plug.

Flat Twin: Flat Twin is an engine configuration where two cylinders lie flat, horizontally opposed. The BMW Boxer engine is the prime example.

Foot Pegs: Foot Pegs are pegs wide enough to support the foot while riding a motorcycle. They may be mounted directly under the rider or placed forward in the Cruiser style. Sometimes, floorboards are used in the place of Foot Pegs.

Forward Controls: The Foot Pegs, rear foot brake pedal, and gear shift on a motorcycle can be located either pretty much straight down from the rider or positioned more to the front of the bike. In a forward position, the controls are referred to as Forward Controls.

Full-Face Helmet: A Full-Face Helmet surrounds the head with protection on the top, sides, back, front, and chin areas. There is a lift-up face shield and usually ventilation ports. Peripheral vision must meet standards so you will be able to see to the side. This helmet is harder to get used to and harder to put on especially if you wear glasses. It does, however, afford the best protection for your head and face should you find yourself sliding across the pavement face down.

Geezer Glide: Geezer Glide is a term used by some old Harley riders to lovingly refer to the Harley full dress (Dresser) Touring Bikes or Baggers.

Get-Off: Sometimes a rider gets into a situation where the motorcycle becomes unstable either because of an impending accident or sudden maneuver and the bike and rider part company. This is called a Get-Off.

Gold Wing: Gold Wing is a Honda motorcycle model first introduced in 1975. It's a Touring Motorcycle suitable for luxurious Two-Up Touring. Many Gold Wing owners belong to the GWRRA.

GPS: These days, motorcyclists want to equip their motorcycles with all the latest electronic gadgets. One of the most useful is a GPS (Global Positioning System). This tiny unit attaches to the handlebars and guides you from any point on the earth's surface to any other point giving you turn by turn instructions based on signals it receives from a set of 24 satellites that are orbiting the earth.

GWRRA: GWRRA stands for the Gold Wing Road Riders Association. This group headquartered in Phoenix, AZ has over 75,000 members worldwide. Members of the GWRRA mainly ride Honda Gold Wing and Honda Valkyrie motorcycles.

Hack: A Hack is another term for a Sidecar. Also called a chair. Hacks are an old form of motorcycle transport that enabled riders to extend their riding season on the relative comfort of 3-wheels instead of two. Hacks are still an important part of the motorcycling scene.

Hard Tail: Hard Tail refers to a motorcycle with no rear suspension. Harley-Davidson motorcycles were all Hard Tails until 1958 when the Duo-Glide was introduced.

Headlight Modulator: A Headlight Modulator is a device that turns your motorcycle headlight into an attention-getter. It makes your headlight beam pulsate 240 times per minute during daylight hours. Modulators are legal in all 50 states of the USA.

Heel-Toe Shifter: Normally, shifting on a motorcycle is done by placing your foot under the shift lever, squeezing the clutch lever all the way to the grip and then kicking upward smartly for each gear change as you from first through all the higher gears. Similarly, downshifting from a high gear to the next lower gear requires the rider to place their foot on top of the shift lever and stomp down smartly to make one gear change.

When a heel-toe shifter is used, the rider has use of a different mechanism designed so that a downward kick is all that is required whether upshifting or downshifting. By stomping down on the ball of your foot on the forward lever, the transmission is shifted into a lower gear. By stomping down on your heel on the rear lever, the transmission is shifted into a higher gear.

Of course, you can also use the heel-toe shifter as a normal shifter. Just use the forward lever and stomp down to go to a lower gear and kick upward on the bottom of the lever with the toe of your boot to go to a higher gear.

Hell's Angels: Movie produced in 1930 by Howard Hughes. Also a B-17 squadron in WWII. The name was subsequently taken by a group of motorcyclists for their motorcycle club. This club has expanded and has many chapters. Their motorcycle of choice is the Harley-Davidson and some feel that the club has dangerous elements. In the public's eye, sometimes every motorcyclist is a member of Hell's Angels.

Helmet Hair: Wearing a motorcycle helmet tends to mess up one's hair. Removing the helmet usually leaves hair sticking out in all directions. This is called helmet hair. It can be minimized by use of special skull caps and liners that hold the hair in place.

Highsiding: Highsiding occurs when the rider of a motorcycle is flipped over the handlebars of the bike. This most often occurs when the rider locks the rear brakes during a panic stop and then releases the brake. This causes the rear wheel to kick the bike upwards throwing the rider off.

Highway Pegs: Footrests situated forward of the rider so the legs can be stretched out to relieve highway fatigue.

HOG: Has various meanings from Harley Owners Group to simply a Harley rider or the machine itself

Hollister Incident: A band of bikers rode into Hollister, CA. on July 4, 1947 for a 3-day rally. Some drunkenness occurred and the press made a sensational story out of it that appeared in Life magazine. Most of the biker movies have perpetuated the Hollister image that appeared in Life. The movie, *The Wild One*, starring Marlon Brando was based on this incident. Even today, motorcyclists are still viewed in the light of Hollister.

Honda Dream: First Honda model that popularized motorcycles to Americans in the early '60s.

Hondamatic: Riders of motorcycles are used to shifting gears and using a clutch. However, some new riders would like to do away with shifting and clutching since they may have become used to automatic transmissions in cars. They often ask if they can buy an Automatic motorcycle. Well, in the late '70s and early '80s, Honda made an Automatic. They called it the Hondamatic. Honda made the CB750A Hondamatic from 1976-1978. They produced the Hawk Hondamatic in 1978. For 1979-1981, Honda produced the CM400A Hondamatic. Finally, in 1982-1983, Honda made the CM450A Hondamatic.

Lately, you can get an automatic on the Boss Hoss or Ridley.

Horsepower: One Horsepower is defined as the amount of work required to raise a 550 pound weight one foot in one second. Horsepower, Torque, and RPM are interrelated by the formula: HP = Torque * RPM/5252.

Hurt Report: Harry Hurt conducted the definitive study on motorcycle accidents at USC in 1979. His team studied 3622 accidents and drew many important conclusions relative to motorcycle safety. This report has been debated ever since mostly by motorcyclists who are divided on the need for motorcycle helmets. No follow-on study has been conducted since then and the helmet debate continues.

Inline 4: An Inline 4 is a motorcycle engine having four cylinders in a row.

Integrated Brakes: Integrated Brakes are used on motorcycles to link together the front and rear brakes. Many inexperienced riders in panic situations tend to overuse the rear (foot) brake. This causes skidding and possible loss of control. Integrated brakes work by applying one of the front disc brakes along with the rear brakes when the brake foot pedal is depressed. The best situation is for a motorcyclist to use the front and rear brakes together to effect a fast controlled stop. With Integrated Brakes, at least there is the improved chance that the bike will stop in a controlled manner just using the rear brake. Bear in mind that proper use of the front brake while applying the rear brake will cause the machine to stop faster.

Iron Butt Rally: The Iron Butt Rally is an 11 day 11,000 mile motorcycle trip around the perimeter of the United States. It has a series of checkpoints that must be visited within a two-hour window.

Jumper Cables: Jumper Cables are heavy electrical cables with clips on the ends used to connect two batteries together to Jump Start a motorcycle Battery.

Jump Start: Jump Start is the term used to describe starting a motorcycle that has a dead Battery by placing a good battery in parallel with the dead battery.

Kickstarter: A Kickstarter is used to start a motorcycle. The kickstarter is a pedal that is swiftly kicked downward to turn over the engine to start the bike. Each motorcycle equipped with a kickstarter may have a different procedure to ensure successful operation. Kickstarters were standard many years ago. Most modern motorcycles have an electric starter.

Kill Switch: The Kill Switch is in series with the ignition switch. When the Kill Switch is open, the bike will not start.

Knucklehead: Knucklehead is the name of the Harley-Davidson engine used from 1936-1947. If you sit on the seat of a knucklehead machine and look down to the right side of the engine, the rocker box looks like the knuckles on your fist. Check out the Harley-Davidson Web site to see pictures of their engines.

Laconia: Large rally and races in Laconia, NH in late June each year. Predominantly, Harley-Davidson riders.

Lane Splitting: Lane Splitting is the process of riding your motorcycle in the same lane with cars or other motorcycles. Normally it is done at low speeds with cars stopped or nearly so. California is a state that does allow it mainly because the California Highway Patrol motorcycle cops, CHP, do it. California regulations say: "Lane splitting by motorcycles is permissible but must be done in a safe and prudent manner."

Laughlin: Laughlin is a motorcycle rally held in Laughlin, Nevada near the Arizona border in late April.

Leathers: Motorcyclists wear their leathers. They wear as much leather as possible to protect them from the elements and the ground, should they fall. This means leather jackets, chaps, gloves, boots, and riding suits. Usually, the leathers are ventilated for cooling.

Left-Turner Accidents: The most frequent motorcycle/automobile accidents are collisions of motorcycles with oncoming left-turning drivers. These Left-Turner Accidents are the leading cause of death of motorcyclists. If you only remember one Motorcycle Views Glossary definition, let it be this one.

Slow down before you enter an intersection. Have an escape route planned. Stay visible. Don't travel too close to cars in front of you. Position your bike so it can be seen by the Left-Turner. Eye contact is not enough.

Don't become a victim to a Left-Turner Accident.

LEO: Cops have many terms that describe them. One term sometimes used by motorcyclists is LEO which stands for Law Enforcement Officer.

Lid: We stress here that riders should always wear a helmet. We want you to maximize your chances of survival when riding. Another name for a helmet is a Lid. Some states require helmet use. Other states have age restrictions. Some states don't require a helmet at all.

My advice is to wear a lid, preferably not a beanie. We want to see you around for many years to come.

Lowsiding: Lowsiding occurs when a motorcycle falls over and drops the rider to the ground. Some riders have been known to deliberately drop their bikes to avoid an accident. This is usually a bad idea since falling off the bike will most likely cause greater injury than staying with the bike and attempting a controlled stop or purposeful maneuver to avoid an accident.

Master Cylinder: A Master Cylinder for a motorcycle is usually located in two places. The front master cylinder is positioned on the right handlebar where the front brake lever can easily activate it to control the front disc brake. The rear master cylinder is located near the rear foot brake pedal.

The Master Cylinder contains a reservoir of brake fluid and controls the movement of fluid through the brake lines to the Caliper assemblies.

M/C: M/C stands for Motorcycle Club. M/C is also written as MC. A motorcycle club is just a group of riders who band together for support and fellowship. Some clubs are independent having no other chapters. Club members often wear what is referred to as "colors," a vest or patch or hat that displays an emblem and other colors that are used by the club to distinguish itself from other clubs.

There are also riding clubs that don't have the special member commitments often found in motorcycle clubs.

There are also large national organizations and associations of riders such as the Gold Wing Road Riders Association (GWRRA) , the Harley Owners Group (H.O.G.), the BMW Motorcycle Owners of America (BMWMOA), the Women on Wheels (W.O.W.), the Motor Maids, and the Women in the Wind (W.I.T.W.). These all have local chapters.

Metric Cruiser: Metric Cruiser is a general category of bikes including Honda, Yamaha, Kawasaki, and Suzuki as opposed to American bikes such as Harley-Davidson and Indian. The American bikes tend to use the English system of measurement: pounds, feet, miles, inches, while the Metric Cruisers use the Metric system of measurement: Kilograms, meters, etc. The fact that some American bikes may use the Metric system to quantify their components may still render them as American rather than Metric, at least in the eyes of the Metric Cruiser enthusiasts. By the way, the Harley-Davidson V-Rod model is also a Metric Cruiser.

Motocross: Motocross is an outdoor dirtbike competition using long courses over basically natural terrain with some manmade jumps. It can be a family sport with mom and dad assisting their young boys and girls learning the basics. Motocross involves racing in what are called Motos. More popular variants of Motocross include Supercross and Arenacross which cater to professional racers, larger audiences, TV, and endorsements.

Motorcycle: A motorcycle is a 2-wheel vehicle patterned after a bicycle but powered with an engine and supported with a much heavier frame. Early motorcycles were actually bicycles fitted with small internal combustion engines. There was a gradual evolution as numerous motorcycle manufacturers entered the market and competed against each other.

A motorcycle works using a complex interrelated set of parts controlled by both hands and feet and requires coordination and skill not required to drive an automobile.

Motorcycles have been a part of transportation for a long time. They were once much more prevalent than automobiles until such pioneers as Henry Ford found out how to mass produce cars at a lower price.

Over the years, the motorcycle has come to fit a variety of needs beyond basic transportation.

Today's rider may use a motorcycle for commuting or everyday use. Some ride as part of their lifestyle. Some ride on lengthy cross-country tours.

Motorcycles have evolved to include 3-wheel vehicles called Trikes. A motorcycle is sometimes fitted with a Sidecar.

In the United States, only one company, Harley-Davidson, has been able to survive over 100 years, producing models every year since its first model in 1903. In fact, to most non-motorcyclists, the words "motorcycle" and "Harley-Davidson" are used interchangeably.

Although many motorcycle brands exist, the most prominent besides Harley-Davidson are Honda, Yamaha, Kawasaki, Suzuki, BMW, and American made Victory.

Also Known As: Scooter, Bike, Scoot, Motorbike

Photo © 2005-2011 Walter F. Kern

Motorcyclist: A Motorcyclist is one who rides a motorcycle or bike. The similar term Biker brings up a different image to most people. There is not as much of a lifestyle change associated with the term Motorcyclist as there is with the term Biker.

Motor Maids: The Motor Maids is a woman's motorcycle organization founded in 1940 by Linda Dugeau of Providence, Rhode Island and Dot Robinson of Detroit, Michigan. Dot was named the first President and remained in that position for the next 25 years. The Motor Maids originally had 51 chartered members. The American Motorcycle Association Charter #509 was issued to the club in 1941.

MSF: MSF stands for the Motorcycle Safety Foundation that sponsors motorcycle training courses and classes.

Naked Bike: A Naked Bike is a motorcycle with little or no wind-deflection and an exposed chassis. The Ducati Monster comes to mind.

Neutral Light: Most modern motorcycles have a green neutral light that lights when the motorcycle transmission is in neutral.

Finding neutral on a bike can be difficult at times. Just watch the light on your instruments. When it turns green, you're in neutral. Make sure you have the ignition on so you can see the light.

Newbie: A Newbie is a person who is just starting to learn about some new endeavor. A Newbie is a beginner or novice. On the Motorcycle Views Web site we use the term Newbie for both new riders and persons who are new to motorcycling.

NHTSA: The National Highway Traffic Safety Administration (NHTSA) is an agency of the United States Department of Transportation (DOT).

OEM: OEM stands for Original Equipment Manufacturer. As an example, Harley makes a motorcycle out of parts and Harley is the OEM for that motorcycle. Users then may modify or add parts to the machine. Most likely the added parts are not OEM but so-called aftermarket parts.

Off-Camber: An Off-Camber turn is one that is banked higher on the inside than on the outside of the turn. Normally roads have a slight crown in the middle to let the rain wash off. However, some roads may have a pronounced crown, making turning left around a curve, a skillful exercise in the Off-Camber world.

Off-Road: Off-Road implies that a motorcycle is ridden off the street onto dirt, trails, sand, woods, hilly terrain, etc. There are also Off-Road motorcycles that have special features to withstand the non-street environment presented by Off-Road riding.

Oil Filter: An Oil Filter filters the oil in the motorcycle engine. Changing the oil and oil filter is one task that many riders do for themselves. Consult your owner's manual for recommended intervals and oil weights to use.

Oilhead: Oilhead refers to the air-cooled engines of more recent BMW motorcycles that also contain an oil cooler.

On Any Sunday: Famous motorcycle movie featuring Malcolm Smith that popularized motorcycling.

One-Off: Those who happen to watch TV shows such as American Chopper get to observe the building of a Custom motorcycle from the ground up. Often these bikes are one of a kind and are sometimes referred to as a One-Off.

One Percenter: Many years ago, the AMA stated that 99% of motorcyclists are law abiding people and only 1% are causing trouble. Those riders who felt they were in that 1% assumed the name One Percenters and started wearing patches denoting themselves as One Percenters.

Outlaw: The AMA attempted to organize most of the motorcycle racing competitions many years ago. Some motorcycle clubs and groups of riders did not want to go along with the AMA rules. They became known as Outlaws since they fell outside the laws of the AMA. After the Hollister Incident in 1947, the concept of the outlaw motorcycle gang began becoming part of the American psyche. The term Outlaw then took on a different meaning. Today, some people view all motorcycle clubs as gangs and assume that all gangs are outlaws. Nothing could be further from the truth.

Packing List: A Packing List is an alphabetical list of items to be taken with you when you travel on your motorcycle. It may contain categories such as Regular Stuff, Clothes, and Toiletries. It might also identify the location on the bike where the article will be stored. If you do much touring on your bike, you'll need to get organized. A packing list is a necessity. My packing list is contained in Appendix 3.

Panhead: Panhead is the name of the Harley-Davidson engine used from 1948-1965. The chromed rocker covers resemble a baking or frying pan.

Paralever: Paralever is the name of a radically different rear suspension system first used on the BMW R100GS motorcycle. The Paralever works on the principle of a parallelogram with a Torque arm that allows the Shaft Drive to move through two angles, giving about 70 percent more rear-suspension travel. There is considerable discussion as to just how this suspension works, but it apparently does and has been used in many other BMW models.

Parallel-Twin: A Parallel-Twin is a motorcycle engine having two cylinders placed parallel to each other and vertical.

Passenger Pegs: Passenger Pegs are pegs wide enough to support the foot of a passenger (Pillion) while riding. They are mounted directly under the passenger. Sometimes, floorboards are used in the place of Passenger Pegs.

Petcock: A petcock is a manually operated device inserted in the gas line that allows for an On, Off, and Reserve position for the gas supply. When the motorcycle starts to sputter, the rider turns the petcock to the Reserve position to gain access to additional gas while a gas station is sought. Some modern motorcycles have gas gauges and automatic gas shutoff systems making the manual petcock unnecessary.

Here's a good reference on Gas Tanks that also discusses all the types of Petcocks: www.dansmc.com/gastank.htm. It discusses ON-OFF-RES, ON-RES-PRI, and ON-OFF systems: Gas Tanks

Pillion: The backseat on a motorcycle for its passenger. Also, a passenger is said to ride pillion. Pronunciation: Pill-yon (noun)

PMS: PMS is defined as Parked Motorcycle Syndrome. This is a common disease that occurs in the winter when a rider is unable to take his/her motorcycle out for a ride and is forced to think about things other than motorcycles.

Pocket Bike: I seem to be inundated with stories about pocket bikes or mini-bikes that are starting to appear everywhere across the USA. These are extremely small bikes that look like miniature sportbikes, have engines under 50cc and sell for prices as low as $200. eBay is loaded with such vehicles. I first saw these at Americade a few years ago ridden down Canada Street by regular motorcyclists. Now, the bikes are getting in the hands of the masses and used on sidewalks and city streets mainly by young people. Pocket bikes are quite low to the ground and can barely be seen by motorists. Although laws are sparse regulating the bikes, local law enforcement officials are clamping down on their use. My advice to you is to watch out for these vehicles. Fortunately, they can usually be heard even if they can't be seen.

Poker Run: A Poker Run is an organized motorcycle event where riders travel over a prescribed course and at designated stopping points, select a card. At the end of the poker run, the person with the best poker hand wins a prize. Motorcycle poker runs usually require a fee to enter with a part of the proceeds going to charity. Some poker runs are done from bar to bar but in the interest of safety, I don't recommend these. The best motorcycle poker runs have a dinner at the end point and only serve soft drinks. Please do not drink and ride your motorcycle. The rules for Poker Runs vary depending on the event.

Polar Bear Grand Tour: Most motorcyclists don't ride in the winter. However, the Polar Bear Grand Tour held each Sunday beginning with the last Sunday in October and ending with the last Sunday in March, allows riders to continue riding throughout the winter in NJ, DE, PA, CT, and NY. (The Polar Bears are continually being confused with those "other" Polar Bears who like to jump in the ocean in the middle of the winter.) Check out the Polar Bear Grand Tour Web site (polarbeargrandtour.com) for additional information, schedules, pictures, and videos.

Poseur: A Poseur is a person who pretends to be what he is not. There are those individuals within motorcycling who are superficially attracted to the image of the biker but who are unwilling to set about the much more difficult task to become a real motorcyclist.

Positive Camber: A Positive Camber turn is one that is banked higher on the outside of the turn than on the inside. NASCAR racetracks and Interstate highways are examples of roads that have Positive Camber.

Powder Coating: There are various ways to paint a motorcycle. A popular method these days is powder coating. The paint mixture is normally sprayed on the surface where it clings by electrostatic attraction.

Pushrods: Pushrods are used to connect to rocker arm assemblies which, in turn, open and close valves. In this case, the Camshaft is located near the crankshaft. The rotation of the camshaft causes its lobes to press upward on the Pushrods which extend to the top of the engine and connect to the rocker arms. Harley-Davidson motorcycles are heavy users of the pushrod method of valve operation.

Rake and Trail: Rake is the angle of the fork away from vertical toward the rider. Trail is the distance on the ground between a vertical line dropped straight down from the center of the wheel and a projection of the fork extended until it touches the ground. As the rake increases, the trail increases. The more rake, the more stable the handling.

Rally: A gathering of motorcyclists. Could be any number as small as 10 or as large as 500,000.

Rat Bike: A rat bike is a bike that is usually unkempt and is loaded with all sorts of luggage, tools, tents, bedrolls, flags, pots and pans, clothes, jackets, etc. You can't miss a rat bike. It has everything on board and looks like the rider has all his or her possessions strapped to the bike.

Rearsets: When racing a motorcycle or just doing the twisties, a rider often finds that the pegs just get in the way when leaning the bike. A way around this is to relocate the pegs, foot brake, and shifter farther back and up on the machine. This is done with special rearsets.

RETREADS®: The RETREADS® Motorcycle Club was conceived and founded in 1969 by five men through a letters column in a motorcycle magazine. In time, the group agreed they should form a correspondence motorcycle club. The RETREADS® became a formal club in July, 1970. Membership requirements are an age of 40 plus (XL+), and a love of motorcycling.

Revolution: Revolution is the name of the Harley-Davidson engine first introduced in the V-Rod in 2001. This engine is an 1130cc, 115 HP, 60 degree V-Twin using rubber mounting with a single counterbalancer. Check out the Harley-Davidson site to see pictures of their engines.

Riceburner: A Riceburner is a Japanese motorcycle. The term tends to be used by riders of American made motorcycles.

Ride Bell: There are many stories about the Ride Bell. Here's one: Have you noticed that small bell on some people's bikes and wondered why it was there? It's more than just decoration. It has a specific function. As we all know, life has many mysteries that have no apparent solutions. One of these is Evil Road Spirits. They are the little gremlins that live on your bike. They love to ride. They're also responsible for most of your bike's problems.

Sometimes your turn signal refuses to work, or the battery goes dead, the clutch needs adjustment, or any of several hundred other things go wrong. These problems are caused by Evil Road Spirits. Road Spirits can't live in the presence of a bell. They get trapped in the hollow of the bell. Among other things, their hearing is extremely sensitive. The constant ringing and confined space of the bell drives them crazy. They lose their grip and eventually fall to the roadway. (Have you ever wondered how potholes are formed?) The bell has served its purpose.

If your bell was given to you, its power is greatly increased, and you know that somewhere you have a special friend helping to look after you. So, if you have a friend that doesn't have a bell, why not be the person to give them one? It's a nice feeling for the recipient to know you personally cared. The bell, plus a good preventive maintenance program by the bike's owner, will help eliminate the Evil Road Spirits.

Ride To Work Day: Ride to Work Day was inspired by various "Work to Ride - Ride to Work" T-shirts, stickers and other marketing materials created between 1989 and 1991 by Andy Goldfine for the Aero Design and Manufacturing Company, otherwise known as Aerostich Riderwear, a Minnesota based manufacturer of motorcycle riders clothing.

In 1992 these items inspired motorcycle magazine editor Fred Rau to write an editorial calling for an annual national ride to work day. That day, the third Wednesday in July, was first celebrated in 1992 and has been celebrated each year since. According to the Ride to Work nonprofit advocacy organization, "Ride to Work Day reveals that motorcyclists come from all walks of life, work in all occupations, and range in age from teenagers to grandparents."

Rigid: A bike with no rear suspension is said to be a rigid. Harley-Davidson motorcycles all had rigid frames until 1958 when the Duo-Glide was introduced. Most Choppers are built using rigid frames.

Rig: A motorcycle with an attached Sidecar. Also any combination of motorcycle with or without sidecar pulling a trailer.

Road Rash: Road Rash is a term used to define injuries to the skin when a rider falls or is thrown from the motorcycle and lands or slides on the pavement. One reason riders wear Full-Face helmets, gloves, leather jackets, Chaps, and boots is to minimize Road Rash. Let the leather suffer the Road Rash.

RPM: RPM is defined as Revolutions Per Minute. Horsepower, Torque, and RPM are interrelated by the formula: HP = Torque * RPM/5252.

RUB: Rich Urban Biker.

Saddlebags: Saddlebags are either soft or hard containers attached over the rear fender of a motorcycle. They hang down on each side of the bike and provide storage for items that are carried on the bike. Usually, saddlebags are made of leather and contain flaps that are fastened to the bag through buckles. These soft saddlebags are fastened to the bike with leather laces or other detachable devices. Hard saddlebags can be plastic, fiberglass, or metal and are usually permanently attached.

Scooter: A scooter, in its purist definition, could be considered a small motorcycle with a step-through or feet-forward design. For bikers, a scooter might just means any motorcycle, sometimes also called a Scoot.

Scoot: Affectionate term for a motorcycle.

SCRC: The Southern Cruisers Riding Club (SCRC) was founded by Rick Perry (Rickster) as a local motorcycle riding club in the Memphis, LA area. Within five years, the club had chapters all over the United States and elsewhere in the world and had over 26,000 members.

Shaft Drive: Shaft Drive is a method to transmit power from the transmission to the rear wheel of the motorcycle using a shaft. The shaft is much like the driveshaft on an automobile. One end connects to the end of the transmission and the other end connects to a sealed ring gear on the rear hub. Shaft-drive systems are trouble free and require lubrication usually only when the rear tire is replaced.

Shovelhead: Shovelhead is the name of the Harley-Davidson engine used from 1966-1985. The shovel engine has rocker boxes, not covers, and rocker arms pivoting on shafts leading to castings on the heads. The whole thing resembles the back of a coal shovel. Check out the Harley-Davidson site to see pictures of their engines.

Sidecar: A Sidecar is attached to a motorcycle to create a 3-wheeled combination. The sidecar is also known as a hack, outfit, rig, or chair. Sidecar combinations have been used for over a hundred years. A sidecar/motorcycle combination is neither a motorcycle nor a car in handling characteristics. Special driving techniques must be mastered before one can safely operate a rig.

Sidestand: The Sidestand retracts from the left side of a motorcycle and contacts the ground to hold up the machine at a slight angle off vertical. In recent years most bikes cannot be started with the sidestand down since there had been so many instances on older bikes where riders rode off with the sidestands still down and accidents occurred.

Sissy Bar: A tall backrest on the passenger seat of a motorcycle. It helps to keep a passenger from falling off and it's also useful to Bungee luggage to a bike when there is no passenger.

Snell Helmet Rating: The Snell Memorial Foundation rates motorcycle helmets. The rating is based on dropping the helmet containing a simulated head from a height of 10 feet. The "head" must receive no more than 285 Gs. A second drop is done from a lower height. See Bill Stermer's book, *Motorcycle Touring and Travel*, for more information.

Soft Tail: A Soft Tail is a motorcycle that appears to have a Hard Tail rear suspension but in reality has shock absorbers that are hidden from view. Harley-Davidson has many Soft Tail models but they call them Softails.

Sportbike: Very fast, colorfully decorated, high-performance motorcycle. Sportbikes are flashy, fast, and lightweight. Some are capable of Sport-Touring.

Sporty: Harley-Davidson introduced the Sportster in 1957. The Sportster is sometimes called a Sporty or Sportie, depending on how you like to spell it. By the way, 2004 was the first year that rubber-mounted engines were used in Sporties, thereby greatly reducing the vibration long a part of the Sportster experience. Alternate Spellings: Sportie

Sportster: Harley-Davidson's entry level model is a popular model for both men and women riders. Also Known As: Sporty, Sportie. This venerable Harley-Davidson model has been around since 1957 and has a legion of devoted fans -- and detractors. It has multiple personalities.

Sport-Tourer: A Sport-Tourer motorcycle is one that is sporty like a Sportbike but capable of Touring with some comfort. The speeds and handling are similar to a sportbike but there is usually storage for traveling and more creature comforts.

Springer: A Springer is a particular Harley-Davidson model in the Softail family. It is characterized by a front fork that uses springs and a shock instead of a telescopic fork. The Springer front fork was first used on a 1948 FL model then abandoned until forty years later when it appeared on the FX Softail line, much improved in performance.

Squid: Have you seen a motorcycle rider who does not wear protective clothing, darts into and out of traffic at high speed, seems to need some motorcycle training and, in general, acts like he/she doesn't know what they're doing? You've seen a Squid. No one is quite sure where this term came from. It is a naval term for a young sailor. It may be an acronym. Some examples are "SQUirrely kID," "Stupid, QUick, and Inevitably Dead," or "Super QUick, Inadequately Dressed."

Standard Bike: Tends to be a motorcycle without frills such as Saddlebags, windshield, radio, or trunk. It is the cheapest to buy and usually has small Rake and Trail.

Stoppie: A stoppie is a motorcycle maneuver performed by a skilled rider to stop a moving motorcycle so the rear wheel is raised in the air while the machine is balanced on the front tire.

Stroker: Stroker has at least two definitions. First, it is another word for a 2-Stroke engine. Second, it refers to increasing the stroke in a Harley-Davidson engine (or any other make) to give it more horsepower. The resulting Harley is called a Stroker.

Sturgis: Town of 6000 in SD where the Sturgis Motorcycle Rally is held in early August. The rally attracts as many as 400,000 motorcyclists to the area.

Supercross: Supercross is a dirtbike competition using relatively short courses inside athletic stadiums with mostly manmade jumps. Supercross has its roots in Motocross and might be considered a step-up in terms of organization, promotion, showmanship, and professionalism.

Swing Arm: Older motorcycles and some new motorcycles have Rigid frames much like bicycles. Thus, the frame is connected directly to the rear wheel. A swing arm is a movable joint between the frame of the motorcycle and the rear wheel assembly. It supports the rear wheel and associated suspension components.

Tachometer: The Tachometer on a motorcycle tells the speed of the engine in revolutions per minute (RPM).

Tailgunner: The last rider in a group formation of motorcycles is called the Tailgunner.

Tank Bag: A piece of luggage that mounts on top of the gas tank of a motorcycle. Sometimes contains a clear plastic top where route directions can be viewed by the rider without stopping.

Target Fixation: A motorcyclist often inadvertently looks at an object and finds himself/herself headed straight for that object. This is target fixation and must be avoided. It's also said that "you go where you look." To avoid an object, don't look at it. Look where you need to go to avoid the object. Avoid target fixation.

Tats: Tats, short for Tattoos. Many bikers have tattoos that depict various aspects of their relationship with their motorcycle or other motorcycle-related activities. The Harley-Davidson logo is a popular element of biker tattoos.

T-Bone: A T-Bone is a category of motorcycle accident where the rider runs head-on into the side of another vehicle. Usually, the other vehicle is a car that has turned left in front of the rider and the rider cannot perform an evasive maneuver or swerve to avoid the car and hits it straight on in the side. The car is the top of the "T" and the motorcycle is the vertical part of the "T."

Telelever: Telelever is the name of a front suspension system used on BMW motorcycles. The front forks are just oil-filled struts. Two ball joints control the suspension through a complex of interacting components. The resulting suspension has received high marks from almost all testers. The front end of the bike will not dive under heavy braking. The combination of Telelever front suspension and Paralever rear suspension has transformed the handling characteristics of BMWs.

The Motor Company: Another common name for Harley-Davidson, INC.

The Wild One: Famous motorcycle movie about the Hollister Incident starring Marlon Brando. Brando rode a Triumph, not a Harley.

Throttle Lock: Manual device fitted to the Throttle of a motorcycle that applies friction to keep the throttle from moving. It's used to temporarily give your hand a rest on long rides.

Throttle: The Throttle on a motorcycle is contained in the right grip on the handlebars. The speed of the engine is controlled by twisting the throttle.

Thumper: A single cylinder four-cycle motorcycle engine is sometimes called a Thumper because of its distinct "thump, thump, thump" sound.

Top End: Top End refers to the top portion of a motorcycle engine including the fuel system, valve covers, heads, cylinders, pistons, valves, rings and other components that support the power generation that propels the machine.

Torque: Torque is a turning or twisting force applied at a distance from the axis of the object. Thus, if you apply a 100 pound force to the end of a 3-foot wrench placed on a nut, you are applying 300 pound-feet of torque.

Touring Bike: Any motorcycle that you can take on a tour. Normally, it has a Fairing, Saddlebags, and requires little maintenance. However, any bike can be used for touring.

Touring: Traveling on a motorcycle to visit what's over the next hill. Carried to extreme, some motorcyclists tour up to 50,000 miles a year.

Tranny: The transmission of a motorcycle, a motorcycle tranny

Trials: Trials, or Observed Trials, is a form of Off-Road racing where the course is made up of a series of observed sections that contain natural obstacles such as mud, water, rocks, and logs. The contestant must ride through the sections losing as few points as possible.

Trike: In general, a 3-wheeled vehicle created by stripping off the rear wheel of a motorcycle and replacing it with two automotive wheels attached to a special differential. The rear section is then covered with fiberglass and painted to match the bike. A trike is classified as a motorcycle in most places since a motorcycle is defined as a motorized vehicle with either two or three wheels.

There are many varieties of trikes. Some are based on car foundations such as the VW trikes. Some are custom made from the ground up. Most current trikes are motorcycle based. Trikes all have three wheels. Most trikes have one wheel in front and two wheels behind. Some trikes have two wheels in front and one wheel behind. Most trikes are steered by a regular motorcycle-style handlebar although you will see trikes that use a steering wheel.

The licensing of a trike is varied. Some areas classify it as a motorcycle. Some classify it as a car. Some place it under a special construction category.

In some states, you need a motorcycle endorsement to ride a trike. In others, a car registration is all that is required. In some, a special trike license is required. Check your local regulations.

Some insurance companies don't know much about trikes. They've heard of Sidecars and list them on policies but trikes are not mentioned. When I registered my trike, the insurance man came out and took pictures of it. He'd never seen one before.

A person riding a trike is sometimes called a triker. There is an organization, Trike Riders International (TRI), devoted to triking. Their mission statement says: "TRI is the worldwide organization for owners and enthusiasts of three-wheeled motorcycle conversions and related motor vehicles based on that concept." TRI has recently been merged into the GWRRA.

Triple: A Triple is a 3-cylinder motorcycle engine.

Twin Cam 88B: Twin Cam 88B is the name of the Harley-Davidson engine first introduced in 2000 in the Softail line. This engine is a 1450cc V-Twin using twin counter rotating balancers to fully cancel primary engine vibration.

Twin Cam 88: Twin Cam 88 is the name of the Harley-Davidson engine first introduced in 1999. This engine is a 1450cc V-Twin using twin cams.

Twisties: Twisties are any series of curves in the road that offer a challenge to a motorcyclist.

Two-up: Two people riding on a motorcycle, a rider and a co-rider. Two-up riding requires that the manufacturer's recommended load carrying capacity not be exceeded. Also, special consideration must be given to training the passenger to assist in the various maneuvers required to safely ride the motorcycle with two onboard.

UJM: UJM stands for Universal Japanese Motorcycle. It was a radical concept in the early '70s. The UJM was a Standard Bike offering an alternative to Harley-Davidson Cruisers, British bikes, and the small Japanese motorcycles. The UJM was smooth, fast, powerful, comfortable and could go places and be reliable. The Honda CB-750 was the first UJM.

VIN: VIN stands for Vehicle Identification Number. It's much the same on a motorcycle as the VIN used to identify a car. Each motorcycle manufacturer seems to have a different coding system for the VIN placed on their motorcycles. The owner's manual or service manual should describe the VIN. Also known as: VIN Number

V-Rod: The Harley-Davidson VRSCA V-Rod is a liquid-cooled, 1130cc V-Twin Cruiser. The engine was designed by Porsche.

V-Twin: A V-Twin is a motorcycle engine having two cylinders placed at an angle to each other in the shape of a V.

Wannabe: A Wannabe is someone who tries obsessively to emulate a person, profession, or activity. There are a lot of motorcycle wannabes in the world today. Some wannabe bikers actually become bikers but many are just drawn to motorcyclists and motorcycle activities temporarily and eventually lose interest.

WERA: The Western Eastern Roadracers Association (WERA) also known as WERA Motorcycle Roadracing, Inc, is one of the oldest and largest national sanctioning bodies conducting motorcycle road races at road courses across the United States.

1999 was the 25th Anniversary for WERA Motorcycle Roadracing.

Wheelie: A wheelie is a motorcycle maneuver performed by a skilled rider to raise the front wheel off the ground and ride only on the rear wheel.

Willie G: Willie G. is short for William G. Davidson, Vice-President of Styling for Harley-Davidson. Willie G. is the grandson of one of the founders, William A. Davidson. He is known everywhere affectionately as "Willie G."

Wind Triangle: A triangular cloth or piece of leather worn around the neck area for wind protection.

WOW: WOW is an acronym for Women on Wheels, a national women's motorcycle association.

Wrench: A wrench is a term used to describe a motorcycle mechanic.

Zen and the Art of Motorcycle Maintenance: *Zen and the Art of Motorcycle Maintenance* is a philosophic book by Robert M. Pirsig. This widely quoted book relates the story of a summer motorcycle trip by a man and his eleven-year-old son. It compares life and philosophy with motorcycle maintenance. You'll want to read this several times.

Appendix 2 - How-Tos

Please bear in mind that these Motorcycle How-Tos are for information only. It is recommended that your application of any How-To be done so as to minimize any adverse results that may occur. You should never assume that your application of a particular Motorcycle How-To will fit both your experience level and the motorcycle you are applying it to.

How to Avoid Accidents on a Motorcycle

One reason people don't ride motorcycles is that they are afraid they will have accidents. Avoiding motorcycle accidents in the first place is your best defense. Here are some simple steps to follow to avoid motorcycle accidents:

- Ride assuming that you and your motorcycle are totally invisible to motorists.
- Leave plenty of space in front and back and to the sides from all other vehicles.
- Anticipate trouble situations and know what to do when you see them.
- Beware of motorists turning left in front of you at intersections. This is a leading cause of injuries to motorcycle riders.
- Slow down as your motorcycle enters an intersection and be prepared to make an evasive maneuver if necessary.
- Never drink or take drugs and try to ride a motorcycle.
- Don't ride if you are on medication that makes you sleepy.
- Avoid riding at night, especially late Saturday night and early Sunday when drunken drivers may be on the road.
- Beware of riding your motorcycle into sun glare.
- Don't try to keep up with your friends who may be more experienced. Know your personal limits.
- Beware of taking curves that you can't see around. A parked truck or a patch of sand may be awaiting you.

- Do not give in to road rage and try to 'get even' with another rider or motorist.
- If someone is tailgating you, either speed up to open more space or pull over and let them pass.

Tips:

- Do not prescribe to the tactic of throwing something on the road behind you to warn a tailgater to back off.
- Take a motorcycle safety course to learn what to look for to avoid accidents.
- Wear protective clothing and a helmet in case you forget these tips and find yourself sliding across a concrete road on your backside.

How to Buy a New Motorcycle from a Dealer

You should buy a new motorcycle from a local dealer in a face-to-face situation. Even though you can save a few bucks by buying a bike 200 miles away, there is nothing like having a dealer close to your house. Here's how to buy a bike from a dealer:

- Know what you want. Your motorcycle should fit your needs and you should look around and compare as much as possible before going in to see the dealer.
- Do your homework. Understand what you want and talk to the salesperson about several different bikes that meet your needs.
- Find out the dealer invoice price. Use an online service such as CycleCost.com to obtain a report on each bike. The dealer will do his best to make 10% total profit on the motorcycle.
- Most common dealer fees are destination charges, setup fees, documentation fees, and taxes. There is no easy way to find out their profit margin on these items but it should be between 5% - 15%.
- The salesperson will also try to sell you extras, for example, an extended warranty and accessories. The dealer makes a little on these too. These are specifically choice-driven. If you want it, you buy it.
- As for trade-ins, do your homework here too. You can go to www.kbb.com (Kelly Blue Book) and find out the price of the vehicle either selling it outright or trading it in.
- If you've decided on a bike and you've done your homework, you'll be ready to negotiate. A dealer wants to make about 10% profit on each deal. This means you may be able to talk them down substantially.
- Most dealers like cash deals. If you cannot pay cash, try to put down a big chunk of change. If financing, the larger the

down payment, the less the monthly payments and the less interest you will pay.

- Get a pre-approved loan from a lending institution so financing will not be a consideration. Often dealers will have low-percentage loans available for certain models. These deals may influence your decision.
- As for getting the most for your current bike, your best move is to sell it privately rather than using it as a trade-in. Try to sell it before you buy the new bike.
- Play hardball with the salesperson. The dealer wants to work with you. If they work with you, give them your other business such as apparel, repairs, and accessories.
- After the deal is nearly done, you can almost always get them to sweeten it. A helmet or jacket can possibly be thrown in since the salesperson has spent a lot of time and doesn't want to lose the sale.

Tips:

- Harley-Davidson dealers have a product in great demand. They tend to fall into two camps: Sell over MSRP with short waiting period; Sell close to MSRP with long waiting period. Above steps may not work.
- For non H-D models in great demand, you may have to pay whatever is asked.

How to Buy a Used Motorcycle

New riders should always start out with a used bike until they get trained and get plenty of practice spread over perhaps a year. Here are some ways to get that bike:

- Buying a bike from an Internet auction is the newest way to buy. The most popular service is eBay.
- Every newspaper has motorcycle want ads. You probably won't have far to travel to see the bike. It will be easy to have a local mechanic check out the bike before you buy it.
- There are many Web sites that offer free want ads for motorcycles.
- Always tell your friends that you are looking to buy. Someone may know someone else who has a bike for sale.
- If you belong to a motorcycle club, announce to the members that you are looking for another bike. Since any bike you buy from a club member will be well known to you, you stand to get a good value.
- You're probably going to be visiting your local dealer anyway so look for good trade-ins. Mention to the salespeople that you are looking for a certain kind of bike. They may work to find a bike for you.

How to Clean a Motorcycle Windshield

If your motorcycle has a windshield, it's a good idea to clean it off first before you ride. You also don't want to damage it in the process. Here's a simple way to clean it:

- If the motorcycle has a centerstand, place it on the stand.
- Get two old terry cloth dish towels.
- Dip the corner of one of the towels in some warm water.
- Use the wet end of the towel to clean the outside of the windshield.
- Clean the side mirrors at the same time.
- Use the dry end of the wet towel to dry the windshield. Use the backside of the towel.
- Set the first towel aside.
- Use the second dry towel to complete the drying.
- Get the first wet towel and use it to clean the inside of the windshield.
- Dry the inside with the dry end of the towel as before.
- Complete the drying with the other dry towel.
- Touch up any bad spots.

Tips:

- Never use any commercial window cleaners on your motorcycle windshield.
- Never use paper towels on the windshield.
- Keep some spare dish towels on your bike to clean the windshield while on a trip.

How to Cross a Metal-Grated Bridge on a Motorcycle

Crossing a metal-grated bridge can be an unnerving operation for a new motorcyclist. Learn the technique here:

- Assume you are riding along and you notice a metal-grated bridge ahead.
- Check the mirrors behind to ensure that no one is tailgating you. If so, open up some space.
- As you approach the bridge, check for oncoming traffic.
- Stay in either the left or right tire track position.
- Slow down a little.
- Downshift at least one gear to match your speed.
- Keep your head up.
- Loosen your grip on the handlebars.
- Relax.
- Enter the bridge.
- You will feel the bike drifting a bit. Maintain steady speed.
- Try to maintain a straight line across the bridge.
- You're across. Congratulations.

Tips:

- Resist the temptation to slow down. Keep a steady speed with your head up.
- Riding across a rain soaked metal bridge can be even more unnerving. Wait until you feel comfortable with the dry ones before attempting this.

How to Enhance Motorcycle Safety before You Ride -- the Pre-Ride Check

Motorcycle safety begins by inspecting your motorcycle before you ride. Never ride without first checking these motorcycle safety items. Your life depends on passing these motorcycle safety checks:

- Move your motorcycle so it has at least five feet of space all around it so you can easily do the motorcycle safety check.
- If the motorcycle has a centerstand, place it on the stand.
- If the motorcycle has a windshield, clean it and check for any defects.
- Turn on the motorcycle ignition so the lights will work.
- Check the high and low beams in the motorcycle headlight.
- Check to see if the taillight works. A motorcycle safety check fails if any step fails.
- Depress the motorcycle brake pedal and check to see if the brake light comes on.
- Squeeze the front brake lever and check to see if the brake light comes on.
- Check the left and right turn signals both front and rear.
- Check the motorcycle horn.
- Run your hand along the sidewalls and portion of the tire that touches the road looking for foreign objects. If you find any, don't ride until fixed. Motorcycle safety checking of tires is important.
- Check the air pressure in the motorcycle tires and set to the specifications for the tire.
- Walk around the motorcycle and check for any loose bolts, antenna mounts, plastic, or other items detracting from motorcycle safety.
- Check the oil level in the motorcycle engine.

- If you have a chain, check that it has proper free play and has been oiled recently.

Tips:

- Always make sure your motorcycle headlight is on and set on high beam during the day. At night, set it to low beam for increased motorcycle safety.
- Check that the Kill switch is off or the motorcycle won't start. This motorcycle safety part is often overlooked.
- If the motorcycle has a gas shutoff petcock, check to make sure it is ON.
- Don't forget your own motorcycle safety. Wear safety vests and always wear protective clothing. Check that clothing items do not touch mufflers and chains.

How to Fix a Flat Tire on a Motorcycle

You come out to your garage to take a ride on your bike and find that you have a nail or screw sticking out of your tire. Maybe this situation happens to you on the road. What do you do?:

- You should have a tire plugging kit with you and a means to inflate the tire after the puncture has been sealed. One particularly good kit is the Stop & Go Tubeless Tire Plug Gun Kit.
- If you own a Honda Gold Wing with an on board air compressor, you'll have no trouble inflating the tire after it has been plugged, assuming that you have also purchased an extension air hose to reach your tires.
- For non-Gold Wing riders, consider carrying CO_2 cartridges to inflate the tire.
- After you get a tire plugged, you have to remember that the repair must be considered temporary. Your safety is most important. Consider buying a new tire.

Tips:

Before you use any tire plugging kit, sit down with the kit and read the instructions carefully and even do a test run to satisfy yourself that you know how to use it.

How to Handle a Motorcycle That Dies in Traffic

There are certain situations where a motorcycle will die in traffic either moving or while stopped at a light. Here are things to look for:

- If the bike has a fuel petcock, switch it to reserve. If fuel is low, it should pick right up again.
- Sometimes riders touch the KILL switch by mistake and shut the bike off. Do a quick check.
- Perhaps you have released the clutch too quickly from a stop and had the transmission in a high gear. That will kill the engine. Restart the bike.
- If none of the above works, get the bike off the road for further checks that may include blown fuses, totally empty gas tank, dead battery, etc.

Tips:

Always carry a cellphone for emergencies.

How to Jump Start Your Motorcycle

Here are some steps to follow to jump start your motorcycle. You may want to copy these steps and include in a Ziploc bag also containing your motorcycle jumper cables:

The subject of jumping a battery is controversial. There are many opinions on the best way to jump start a dead battery on a motorcycle. Bike electrical systems are not the same and those differences can cause problems. The best course of action might be to call for a tow truck and get a new battery.

- Arrange another motorcycle so its good battery is close to the dead battery.
- Attach one red clip (+) of the jumper cables to the positive (+) terminal of the dead battery.
- Attach the other red clip (+) to the positive (+) terminal of the good battery.
- Attach one black clip (-) to the frame of the bike with the dead battery or to the negative (-) terminal of the dead battery if a suitable frame location cannot be found.
- Attach the other black clip (-) to the frame of the bike with the good battery or to the negative (-) terminal of the good battery if a suitable frame location cannot be found.
- Start the bike with the dead battery. As soon as it starts, remove the jumper cables in the reverse order that they were attached.

Tips:

- If you use a car battery for the good battery, use the same procedure as above except DO NOT START THE CAR OR HAVE IT RUNNING. Incompatibilities between the car and motorcycle electrical systems may destroy some of the electrical components.

- If you have a roadside assistance plan for your bike, use your cellphone to call for help. You may have to wait an hour or so before help arrives. Many plans will tow you to the nearest bike dealer for your make.
- If you can't get the bike started, you'll need to use the cellphone to summon help. A hat and water bottle will be essential if you encounter a long wait in the sun.

What You Need:

- Motorcycle jumper cables
- Water bottle
- Cellphone
- These instructions

How to Lube a Motorcycle Chain

Consult the owner's manual for your bike for any recommendations on chain oiling made by the manufacturer. In the absence of such recommendations, consider the following as guidelines:

- Your motorcycle chain doesn't need much cleaning if you just ride on normal streets. WD-40 and a rag is about all you need and even then not very often.
- If you use gear oil, oil the warm chain after your last ride of the day using a brush (not an oil can). Put something under the chain to catch the drips and wipe off excess with a rag. Let sit overnight.
- If you use WD-40, spray on warm chain any time. Give it a couple of minutes to drip off or wipe off excess with rag. Ride anytime. Fly-off is moderate.
- If you use spray-on lubes, be sure to spray onto a warm chain. Do not over saturate. Spray it on the inside of the chain. That way on your next ride it will be slung outwards, through the chain.
- For O-ring chains, lube the chain hot. Spray PJ1 Blue Label chain lube directly at the center of the rollers at the rear of the rear sprocket. Move the rear wheel slowly and continue to apply. Let it dry.
- Clean-up: Oil and WD-40 are the easiest to clean up but also can create the biggest fly-off mess. PJ lubes or Chain Wax leaves the least amount of fly-off, but can build up on the chain itself.
- Chain lubing is another of many reasons why you shouldn't buy a bike without a centerstand.

Tips:

Quick Tip: Warm the chain, lube every 500 miles, don't get any on the tires, ride bike right after to work it in, and remove excess after your first ride.

How to Pack a Motorcycle for a Trip

Packing a motorcycle for a trip is more of a challenge than packing your car. This procedure is geared for one motorcycle rider. If you have a co-rider, you'll probably need a trunk or other external trunk behind the passenger:

- Create a packing list of everything you want to take and where it will be placed on the bike. See my Packing List in Appendix 3.
- Depending on the bike, you'll need saddlebags, a tailpack, possibly a tank bag, and at least 3 bungee cords.
- Clothes should be tightly rolled up to assume the smallest space.
- Use the packing list to place items in the various storage areas. Include your jacket as a storage area.
- Evenly distribute the load on the left and right sides. Weigh the bags on a scale.
- Don't put too much weight on the back of the bike. See your owner's manual for limits.
- After all necessities are loaded, place your rain gear somewhere on top of the bike secured by bungee cords. You don't want to have to unpack when it starts to rain.
- Double check your list to ensure that everything is on-board.
- Place the packing list in your jacket or other readily available spot.
- Have a great trip!

Tips:

- Use removable bags in your saddlebags to be able to easily move the contents from your bike to a motel or campsite.
- Always place items you don't want to get wet in plastic zip-type bags.

- Try to keep items you need on the road in a place where they can be easily accessed.

How to Park a Motorcycle

Parking a motorcycle safely depends on the parking surface, inclination and traffic exposure. Here are a few tips on how to position a motorcycle so it can be easily ridden off and be in a visible position:

- Leave the motorcycle parked at an angle to the curb to allow it to be easily pulled into traffic.
- Leave the motorcycle parked with the tire against the curb and in gear.
- Parking a bike where the lean on the sidestand is going DOWN a hill could make the bike unstable and make it difficult to upright from its sidestand. You may want to park near a 35 degree angle to the curb.
- Parking a bike where the lean on the sidestand is going UP a hill could make the bike easy to tip over. You will need to park closer to a 45-50 degree angle from the curb.
- You will need to try various positions on a hill depending on whether the hill is going up or down. Satisfy yourself that the bike remains stable, is easy to lift off its sidestand and is easy to ride away.
- When parking in a parking lot, place the bike in the middle of the lane so that it is parked at the end of the space so motorists will be able to see you as soon as they attempt to park there.
- Know the local parking rules. Sometimes only one motorcycle may be parked in a space. Other places may allow several bikes to use the same parking space to conserve space.
- Be aware of the surface you are parking on. Loose gravel, hot asphalt, sand, and grass may cause your bike to sink on the sidestand. Use a flat plate under the sidestand to better support the bike.

How to Ride a Motorcycle Trike

Learning to ride a motorcycle trike is not as easy as it looks. Here are some pointers to get you going as a triker:

- The motorcycle trike controls are exactly the same as on a motorcycle. However, the steering is different and you need to get used to it.
- Start out driving the trike in a parking lot with your right hand in your back pocket. Leave the trike in first gear, steer it around the lot and do some figure-8s. Get used to the long pushes to turn corners.
- You steer a trike much like a car. You will find it easiest to use a push-pull steering technique. That is, when you want to turn right, pull the right grip toward you while pushing the left grip away from you. Similarly, for a left turn, pull the left grip toward you while pushing the right grip away from you. This technique is especially useful making turns on twisties. You will find it much easier to pull the grip on a hard turn than trying to only push the grip.
- You need to spend some time getting familiar with steering and evasive maneuvers. Your mind will keep telling you that you are on a bike. Train yourself to steer, not countersteer.
- Don't try to put your foot down when you stop. The rear wheel will run over it.
- Remember that the trike is wide and you have to compensate when you pull in next to a gasoline island or a toll plaza.
- Drive the trike in a traffic lane positioned much like a car.
- Turning long sweepers will be easy. Doing twisties will take some technique and a certain amount of muscle.
- Trikes can be altered to have more rake. This makes steering easier but judgment mistakes are easier to make too.

- Tight turns or decreasing radius turns on entrance and exit ramps are noticeably more difficult and require steady pressure.

Tips:

Do not assume that since you've been riding motorcycles for 30 years, that you already know how to ride a trike. You may find yourself in the ditch.

How to Ride a Motorcycle at Night

Riding a motorcycle after dark takes additional skills. Here are some things to think about before you enter the darkness on two wheels:

- Motorists can barely see a motorcycle during the day. Expect to be nearly invisible at night unless you are riding a white bike loaded with extra lights.
- Plan your motorcycle trips to minimize night riding. As you get older you'll find that your vision may become another reason not to ride at night.
- Ride with your low beam on at night but be ready to use the high beam to see farther down the road.
- Wear reflectors on your helmet and jacket.
- If you have loud pipes, be more sensitive of the noise level as the evening wears on.
- Be sure to wear clothing that will keep you warm as the temperature drops.
- Be sure to carry a cellphone and small flashlight on the bike.
- Be wary of animals darting out in front of you, especially deer. Be prepared to stop completely if necessary to avoid being struck by a deer.
- Drunk drivers will be on the road with you. Try to be ready to avoid them. Also, don't drink and ride -- ever.
- Be careful rounding unfamiliar curves where loose gravel or sand may await you.
- Avoid bad areas where residents may attempt to steal your bike or do you harm under the cover of darkness.

Tips:

Wait until you become a proficient motorcycle rider during the day before you attempt to ride after dark.

How to Ride a Motorcycle in a Crosswind

Riding a motorcycle in a crosswind can be a harrowing experience. Here are a few tips:

- Relax your grip on the motorcycle handlebars.
- Keep your head up.
- Let the motorcycle correct itself. You don't have to fight it or white-knuckle it.

Tips:

- Sudden gusts are the worst. Just relax your grip.
- Steady winds such as encountered on the Plains just require fortitude to continue on.
- If there is a lot of oncoming traffic, consider riding in the right tire-track.

How to Ride a Motorcycle in the Winter

You have your own reason for wanting to continue to ride when it gets cold. However, there are some things you need to know if you are determined to ride your motorcycle in the winter, and survive:

- Get a windshield for your motorcycle. Many think a windshield spoils the beauty of the bike. However, riding in 20 degree temperatures with severe wind chill factors will change your mind about getting that windshield.
- Many motorcycle batteries won't last more than two years. Winter riding puts even more strain on a battery. Use a product like Battery Tender to keep it charged.
- Use proper oil. Usually 10W - 40 weight oil designed for motorcycles is sufficient.
- If you have a liquid-cooled bike, be sure that the reading on the anti-freeze is sufficient for the temperatures you expect.
- Make sure the bike has been thoroughly inspected for any mechanical problems. There is nothing more frustrating than being stranded in 20 degree temperatures because of a breakdown.
- Get the proper attitude. You will need to be covered up and motorists will not be expecting to see a motorcycle. Be prepared for additional risks.
- If you plan to travel any distance from home, check out the weather forecasts over the route you'll be taking. It may be clear at home but icy and snowy elsewhere on your route.
- You need to cover your body and eliminate places where the cold air can easily enter. Some riders have been known to wear heavy clothing and seal up openings with duct tape.
- Many riders just dress in layers much as a skier does. There comes a time when most will get tired of being so cold and opt for some electric clothing. Electric vests, gloves, chaps and socks are available.

Tips:

- Winter riding can be fun and safe. Just make sure that both you and your motorcycle are prepared.
- If you opt for electric apparel, be sure to get a thermostat to control the delivery of heat.
- Learn how 550 riders keep warm and have fun as they ride in the Polar Bear Grand Tour (polarbeargrandtour.com) each winter.

How to Ride a Motorcycle in Heavy Traffic

Here are some simple steps that will help you as you venture into heavy traffic on your motorcycle:

- First, pass a motorcycle safety course and get your motorcycle license.
- Ride with an experienced motorcycle rider as you gain experience.
- Ride your motorcycle on safe suburban streets first.
- Next, venture across busy highways without riding on them.
- Then ride on local lightly traveled divided highways.
- Next ride at high-speed on lightly traveled Interstate highways.
- Continue to gradually increase your riding under heavier and heavier traffic situations.
- Do not venture out into heavy traffic until you have mastered all basic motorcycle skills.
- Maintain the 2-second rule at all times.
- Keep scanning 5-6 cars ahead for possible problems.
- Check your rear-view mirrors often.
- Don't ride next to other cars and trucks.
- Ride in the left tire track if alone.
- At a stop, do not ride up to the bumper of the car in front of you. Leave room to escape if necessary.

Tips:

- Take time to learn riding in traffic. As indicated in the steps, learn gradually.
- Always assume you are invisible to other drivers and protect yourself at all times.

- Always wear protective clothing and a helmet until you are experienced. After that, you may have a legal option with the helmet.

How to Sell Your Motorcycle

You've been riding your motorcycle for a few years and now you want a new or different bike. You finally know what you want and are ready to buy. That means you may want to sell your current motorcycle:

- You may opt to keep your motorcycle. If money's no object, you can afford the insurance, and you have the room, then this choice may make sense. Of course, your attachment to the bike may make this the only choice.
- If you're buying a new motorcycle, your dealer will probably take your bike as a trade-in. Be sure to check the various Price Services to see what your bike is worth to help you in the negotiation process.
- Auctioning a bike is a new way to sell your bike. eBay is the most popular service. Check out how others have written up their bikes and included pictures before you decide how to list yours.
- Always tell your friends that you want to sell your motorcycle. Even a friend who doesn't ride might suddenly take an interest in wanting to learn to ride and might want to buy it.
- If you belong to a motorcycle club, group, or association, announce that you want to sell your motorcycle. If there is a club newsletter, list it there also. Since your bike will be well known to the club, you may get a fast sale.
- Often a local dealer will either put your bike on the floor for sale and take a small commission or make it known to others looking for bikes that you have one for sale.
- Every newspaper has motorcycle want ads. Just try to make your ad stand out.
- There are many Web sites that offer want ads for motorcycles.
- You can also try listing on the various motorcycle forums.

How to Shift Gears on a Motorcycle

Shifting gears on a motorcycle is a complex operation. Shifting is done as only one part of operating a bike. All aspects are not covered here. This gives only the basics of motorcycle shifting:

- Get on the motorcycle.
- Retract the sidestand.
- Start the engine in neutral.
- Squeeze the clutch lever with your left hand all the way to the grip.
- Place your left foot on the gear shifter and kick straight down to first gear.
- Give a little throttle with your right hand. Don't race the engine.
- Slowly release the clutch with your left hand while maintaining engine speed with your right hand on the throttle.
- Balance the bike and move off slowly.
- After you are moving and balanced, put your left toe under the gear shifter.
- Squeeze the clutch and release tension on the throttle a little.
- Smartly kick upward with your toe on the bottom of the gear shifter. You are now in second gear.
- Release the clutch smoothly and simultaneously apply more throttle.
- As you gain more speed, repeat the above steps for third, fourth, and fifth gears.
- Downshifting is done similarly except you sharply kick down on the gear shifter to go to the next lower gear.
- As you come to a stop, squeeze the clutch and kick down on the gear shifter, one gear at a time, timing it so you are in first gear as you stop.

Tips:

- Practice use of the clutch and throttle together so as not to stall the engine.
- If you should stall the engine, make sure you have the front wheel straight ahead. Otherwise, you will fall.
- Practice getting the gear shifter into neutral while stopped. Neutral is between first and second gear.

How to Start a Motorcycle

To start a motorcycle is a simple operation. Starting a motorcycle is not the same for all motorcycles but all variations of starting are covered here:

- Get on the motorcycle.
- Retract the sidestand.
- Insert the key in the ignition of the motorcycle.
- Locate and turn ON the fuel petcock. Some motorcycles don't have a need for this step.
- Pull the choke all the way out unless the motorcycle has been running previously.
- Turn the key in the ignition to the ON position.
- Make sure the kill switch of the motorcycle is set to RUN.
- Make sure the motorcycle gear shifter is in neutral.
- Squeeze the motorcycle clutch lever with your left hand all the way to the grip.
- Press the start button with your right thumb.
- Let the starter motor turn over until the engine fires before you release the start button.
- The motorcycle engine should be running at a fast idle.
- Over a period of a few minutes, gradually push the choke in as the motorcycle engine warms up.
- You have started the motorcycle and are ready to go!

Tips:

- If the motorcycle engine fires and then immediately stalls, just press the start button again until it fires a second (or third) time.
- If engine does not start, recheck the kill switch and the fuel petcock.
- Modern motorcycles will stall if you attempt to put the bike in gear while the sidestand is down.

How to Start a Motorcycle on a Grade or Hill

One of the hardest things to master for a beginning rider is how to ride up a grade from a standing start. Many motorcycle driving tests require you to demonstrate this skill. It takes practice:

- Assume you have stopped the bike on an upward grade, that the bike is in first gear, the clutch is pulled in, your left foot is down supporting the bike, and your right foot is depressing the foot brake.
- Check the traffic from left to right looking for a sufficiently long window for you to proceed.
- Keep your right foot on the brake.
- Twist the throttle to get some engine speed.
- Gradually release the clutch to the point where you feel the bike wants to go forward and the bike is at the 'power point.'
- Slowly release the foot brake and note that the power point is keeping the bike from rolling backwards.
- Give one last look both left and right and ahead to make sure you are clear to go.
- Give more throttle and release the clutch a little more to gain forward momentum.
- Balance the bike and move up the incline in first gear. If you release the clutch too quickly, the engine will die and if you aren't alert, you'll drop the bike.
- Once you are moving smoothly, you can proceed through the gears as appropriate.

Tips:

- This procedure should be practiced over and over on a quiet suburban street where you can find a steep incline. It may take a few days of practice to master the skill.

- If you release the clutch too quickly and kill the engine, be prepared for how to get the bike started again.
- Mastering the power point in this exercise so that you have low-speed control of the bike, will save you in numerous other situations.

How to Store Your Motorcycle for the Winter - Winterize

There are many opinions on what should be done to prepare your motorcycle for winter. Here is a basic set of steps to winterize:

- Check over the motorcycle for any mechanical problems.
- Change the engine oil and oil filter.
- Clean and wax the motorcycle.
- Fill the gas tank, add stabilizer according to the instructions on the can, and run the bike for a few minutes.
- Check the battery, clean the battery terminals, and connect a Battery Tender or similar trickle-charger.
- Cover the bike. If possible, keep the bike in a warm garage.
- Make sure the bike is locked up and the registration and other papers along with the key are removed in case the bike is stolen.

How to Tighten a Spark Plug on Your Motorcycle

Most do-it-yourself motorcycle mechanics change their own spark plugs. Most also don't know how much to tighten them to seat properly:

- Ensure that the area around the spark plug hole is clean before removing the old plug.
- Make sure the threaded area of the new plug is clean and dry. Resist placing any oil or WD-40 on the threads.
- Insert the plug making sure that it is threading correctly. You don't want to damage the hole by cross-threading.
- Tighten with your fingers until you feel the crush washer starting to seat at the bottom.
- Tighten 1/4 to 1/2 turn more.

Tips:

If you have a torque wrench and can find a specification in your owner's manual as to how much to tighten the spark plugs, use that value with your torque wrench to tighten the plug.

How to Trip a Traffic Light with a Motorcycle

Every motorcyclist has pulled up to a red traffic light and waited to get the bike to trip a sensor to activate a left-turn or green traffic light. Often they just do not trip. Here are some things to try:

- Get off your motorcycle and push the "walk" button if it is safe.
- Sometimes you may just have to look both ways and run the light. In some places it's OK to "proceed with caution" after 15 minutes, in some places after 2 cycles. You need to know what the law is in your area.
- If you fail to trigger the switch, wait at least one more cycle and then proceed when it is safe.
- Sometimes it helps to kill the engine and restart it just to get the magnetic fields going over the tripping device. Put yourself right over the detector in the pavement. Give the bike a couple of good revs.
- Turn right and then do a "U" turn when you can.
- As you approach the intersection, there are lines cut into the pavement where the sensor was put in. The sensor pad is octagonal or square. Put the most metal over the intersection of two sides.
- Another trick is to put out your kickstand. If you can get the kickstand out, there is more of a metal area to detect. Of course, that will usually also kill the engine. Don't forget to retract your kickstand and restart the bike when the light finally changes.
- Rig your bike with an electro-magnet under the frame. This is wired into the brake lamp circuit and induces enough of a field to trip most lights.
- Consider the purchase of a device that will trip the light for you. Two such products are the Green Light Trigger and the Red Light Changer.
- A new trend is the introduction of special motorcycle boxes that show you where to stop your bike to trip the light. The

front-most "box" has additional diagonal lines, with a bike icon painted in the box.

- Roll forwards and back in an effort to trip the sensors.
- If you are waiting for a left-turn signal light to change, you can always proceed through the intersection on green and make three successive right-hand turns. This only works with regular city blocks.
- Some states have sensors in the lights that can detect flashing lights of police cars and ambulances, and will quickly change the light. You might try flashing your lights to see if that will trip it but don't count on it.
- Threaten legal action. Start by calling the street department and complaining. Every week re-check the light. If you get no action, send them a nice professional letter threatening them with a lawsuit.

Appendix 3 - Packing List

The following packing list may not render too well so, please visit the same Packing List on the Motorcycle Views Web site (motorcycleviews.com/general/paklist.htm). It can be printed out on the Web site.

Note: L = Left saddlebag, **R**= Right saddlebag, **T**= Top Case/Rack/Trunk, and **J** = Jacket

Motorcycle Packing List from Motorcycle Views								
	Where Stored on Motorcycle							
	Rider				Co-Rider			
Item	L	R	T	J	L	R	T	J
REGULAR STUFF:								
Balaclava								
Bungee nets/cords								
Camera, camcorder								
Cell Phone								
Cleaner for bike								
Cover								
Credit Cards								
Duct tape								
Ear plugs								
Electric Vest & Cntl.								
Face Shield Spare								
Fanny Pack								
First Aid Kit								
Flashlight								

Flat Kit							
Gloves(heavy)							
Gloves(light)							
Handy-Wipes							
Helmet Screws(extra)							
Laundry Bag							
Leather Wind Triangle							
Lip Balm							
Lock for Helmet							
Maps / GPS							
Money							
Notebooks							
Packing List							
Plastic Bags							
Rags							
Rainsuit/Boots/Gloves							
Recorder & Tapes							
Sidestand Plate							
Suntan Lotion							
Swiss Army Knife							
Tailpack							
Tire Gauge							
Tools							
Towels for Bike							
Vacation Guides							
Water Bottle							
Weather Radio							

Motorcycle Packing List from Motorcycle Views							
	Where Stored on Motorcycle						
	Rider				Co-Rider		
Item	L	R	T	J	L	R	T	J
CLOTHES:								
Bandana								
Denim Jacket								
Handkerchiefs								
Hat								
Jeans								
Shirts(short-sleeve)								
Shirts(long-sleeve)								
Shorts								
Sneakers								
Socks(regular)								
Socks(riding)								
Swim Shorts/Suit								
T-Shirts(riding)								
Turtleneck								
Umbrella								
Underwear Briefs								
Underwear T-Shirts								
Underwear(thermal)								

Motorcycle Packing List from Motorcycle Views							
Where Stored on Motorcycle							
	Rider				Co-Rider		
Item	L	R	T	J	L	R	T	J
TOILETRIES:								
After-Shave								
Aspirin								
Bandaids								
Clippers								
Comb								
Cosmetics								
Cotton Balls								
Deodorant								
Eye Drops								
Eyeglass Cleaner								
Face creams								
Hairbrush								
Hair Dryer								
Insect Bite Lotion								
Medications								
Mineral Lotion								
Nail File								
Neosporin								
Pre-Shave								
Scissors								
Shampoo								
Shaver								
Soaps								
Toothbrush								

Toothpaste								

20646380R00109

Printed in Great Britain
by Amazon